Longman School
Shakespeare

Sandra 12C
Gustafson

NEW EDITION
for **GCSE**

D1390479

Macbeth

Editor: John O'Connor
Textual Consultant: Dr Stewart Eames

Volume Editor: John O'Connor

GCSE Assessment Practice:
Chris Sutcliffe (AQA)
Pam Taylor (Edexcel)
Margaret Graham (WJEC)
John Reynolds (OCR)

Longman
Part of Pearson

Longman is an imprint of Pearson Education Limited, a company incorporated in England and Wales, having its registered office at Edinburgh Gate, Harlow, Essex, CM20 2JE. Registered company number: 872828

www.pearsonschoolsandfecolleges.co.uk

Longman is a registered trademark of Pearson Education Limited

First published 2004
This new edition published 2010

12
IMP 10 9 8 7

British Library Cataloguing in Publication Data
A catalogue record for this book is available from the British Library

ISBN 9781408236864

Typeset by Juice Creative Ltd, Hertfordshire
Cover photo © Arenapal: Henrietta Butler
Printed in China (SWTC/07)

We are grateful to the following for permission to reproduce copyright photographs:

Getty Images: *page 195*: Andrea Pistolesi/The Image Bank

Every effort has been made to contact copyright holders of material reproduced in this book. Any omissions will be rectified in subsequent printings if notice is given to the publishers.

CONTENTS

ACT 1: SCENE BY SCENE

1 Three Witches plan to meet Macbeth.

2 King Duncan learns that rebels and invaders have been defeated. Macbeth is praised for his bravery in battle, and Duncan names him Thane of Cawdor.

3 The three Witches appear to Macbeth and Banquo. They tell Macbeth that he will become Thane of Cawdor and King of Scotland. They also tell Banquo that his sons will be Kings. After this Macbeth hears that he has been made Thane of Cawdor and he begins to imagine that he can become King.

4 King Duncan names his son Malcolm heir to the throne. Macbeth sees this as an obstacle to his ambition.

5 Lady Macbeth reads a letter from Macbeth telling her what the Witches have predicted. She decides to persuade Macbeth to kill Duncan so that he can become King. Macbeth arrives and tells her that Duncan will be staying at their castle.

6 King Duncan and Banquo arrive at Macbeth's castle. They are greeted by Lady Macbeth.

7 Macbeth debates whether he should kill Duncan. Lady Macbeth persuades him to.

ACT 2: SCENE BY SCENE

1 Macbeth sees a vision of a bloodstained dagger. It seems to be guiding him to kill King Duncan.

2 Macbeth has killed the King. He is so shaken that he has forgotten to leave the bloody daggers near Duncan's attendants so they will be blamed for the murder. Lady Macbeth takes control and returns the daggers to the room.

3 Macduff and Lennox arrive. Macduff discovers the King is dead. Macbeth admits to killing Duncan's attendants because he was so angry that they had murdered the King. Duncan's sons, Malcolm and Donalbain, escape fearing that they will be killed too.

4 Macduff reports the belief that the attendants killed Duncan on the orders of his two sons. Macbeth is to be crowned King.

ACT 3: SCENE BY SCENE

1 Banquo suspects that Macbeth killed Duncan. Macbeth plans to have Banquo and his son Fleance murdered.

2 Macbeth is troubled and anxious. He hints to Lady Macbeth that something is going to happen, but doesn't tell her of his plans to kill Banquo.

3 The murderers kill Banquo, but his son Fleance escapes.

4 Macbeth sees Banquo's ghost at a banquet. He is clearly terrified. He decides to visit the Witches.

5 The Witch goddess, Hecate, is angry with the Witches for leaving her out of their dealings with Macbeth. She promises that Macbeth's confidence in what the Witches show him will be used to destroy him.

6 Lennox and another lord talk about the murders and their suspicions of Macbeth's guilt. They have news that Macduff is with Malcolm in England, planning to return with an army to defeat Macbeth.

ACT 4: SCENE BY SCENE

1 Macbeth visits the Witches again. Their magic apparitions tell him to beware of Macduff, but also that he cannot be killed by a man born of a woman and that he is safe until Birnam Wood marches against him. Macbeth hears from Lennox that Macduff has fled to England.

2 Lady Macduff and her children are murdered on Macbeth's orders.

3 In England, with English help, Malcolm and Macduff plan to get their revenge on Macbeth. Scotland must be freed from the suffering he has caused.

ACT 5: SCENE BY SCENE

1 Lady Macbeth is seen sleepwalking, trying to wash blood from her hands. Her actions suggest that her mind is tormented by what she has done.

2 A number of Scottish lords march to join forces with Malcolm and his English army near Birnam Wood.

3 Macbeth hears that Malcolm's troops are coming to get him. He is unafraid because of his confidence in the Witches' predictions.

4 At Birnam Wood Malcolm's soldiers cut branches from the trees to disguise their numbers as they approach Macbeth's castle.

5 Macbeth hears that Lady Macbeth is dead. He is then told that Birnam Wood seems to be moving. Desperate, he decides to lead his soldiers out and fight to the end.

6 Malcolm's army, led by Siward and his son, gets ready to attack.

7 Macbeth kills young Siward, but troops enter his castle. Macduff hunts for Macbeth.

8 Finding Macbeth, Macduff reveals that he was not born of a woman, but by a Caesarean. Macbeth, knowing that this is the end, still fights desperately. Macduff kills him.

9 Macduff enters with Macbeth's head on a pole. All declare their support for Malcolm, the new King of Scotland.

CHARACTER OVERVIEW

THE ROYAL HOUSE OF SCOTLAND

DUNCAN
King of Scotland
He is murdered by
Macbeth.

MALCOLM
Duncan's elder son
He flees to England
after Duncan is
murdered. He becomes
King of Scotland after
Macbeth.

DONALBAIN
Duncan's younger son
He flees to Ireland
after Duncan is
murdered.

MACBETH'S HOUSEHOLD

MACBETH
Thane of Glamis
He is a general in Duncan's
army and related to
Duncan. He becomes
Thane of Cawdor, then
King of Scotland.

LADY MACBETH
Wife of Macbeth
She helps Macbeth to plan
Duncan's murder and later
commits suicide.

PORTER
*Gatekeeper at
Macbeth's castle*
A comic, drunken figure.

DOCTOR
*In Macbeth's
castle*

SEYTON
*Macbeth's armour
bearer*

GENTLEWOMAN
*Lady Macbeth's
servant*

MURDERERS
*Killers of Banquo, Lady
Macduff and her son*

MACDUFF'S HOUSEHOLD

MACDUFF
Thane of Fife
He is suspicious of
Macbeth and flees
to England. He gets
revenge for the
murder of his family by
killing Macbeth.

LADY MACDUFF
Wife of Macduff
She is murdered at
Macbeth's orders.

SON OF MACDUFF
A boy also murdered at
Macbeth's orders.

BANQUO'S HOUSEHOLD

BANQUO
General in King Duncan's army and a friend of Macbeth
He is murdered at Macbeth's orders.

FLEANCE
Banquo's son
He escapes the murderers sent to kill him by Macbeth.

OTHER THANES AND THEIR HOUSEHOLDS

ROSS
He serves Macbeth but later deserts him. He informs Macduff of his wife's murder.

LENNOX
He serves Macbeth but later switches sides to fight against him.

ANGUS

CAITHNESS

MENTEITH

THE SUPERNATURAL WORLD

THREE WITCHES
They prophesy the future for Macbeth who comes to rely on them for their powers.

HECATE
The Witch Goddess
She is accompanied by three more Witches.

THE ENGLISH

SIWARD
The Earl of Northumberland
He is commander of Malcolm's English army.

YOUNG SIWARD
Siward's son
He is killed by Macbeth in battle.

ENGLISH DOCTOR
At the court of King Edward the Confessor

CHARACTER LIST

THE SUPERNATURAL WORLD

> *Three* WITCHES
>
> HECATE *the Witch goddess* (*with three more Witches*)
>
> APPARITIONS

THE ROYAL HOUSE OF SCOTLAND

> DUNCAN *King of Scotland*
>
> MALCOLM *his elder son*
>
> DONALBAIN *his younger son*

THE MACBETHS' HOUSEHOLD

> MACBETH *Thane of Glamis*
>
> LADY MACBETH *his wife*
>
> *a* PORTER
>
> *a* DOCTOR
>
> SEYTON *Macbeth's armourer*
>
> *Lady Macbeth's* GENTLEWOMAN

OTHER THANES (LORDS) AND THEIR HOUSEHOLDS

BANQUO *a general in Duncan's army*

FLEANCE *his son*

MACDUFF *Thane of Fife*

LADY MACDUFF *his wife*

their young SON

LENNOX

ROSS

MENTEITH } *other Scottish noblemen*

ANGUS

CAITHNESS

THE ENGLISH

SIWARD *Earl of Northumberland*

YOUNG SIWARD *his son*

a DOCTOR *in King Edward's court*

OTHERS

a CAPTAIN *in Duncan's army*

MURDERERS

an OLD MAN

LORDS, ATTENDANTS, SERVANTS, MESSENGERS, SOLDIERS

Scenes are set in Scotland, apart from Act 4 Scene 3, which takes place in England, at the court of King Edward.

In this scene ...

• The three Witches plan to meet Macbeth on the heath, as he returns from battle.

Performance and staging

• In the Roman Polanski film, the Witches are shown burying a severed hand during this scene. If you were the director, what would you have them do?

Themes and issues

• **Deceit and equivocation**: The Witches declare that 'Fair is foul, and foul is fair' (line 11). What do you think they mean?

Context

• In Shakespeare's time, witches were taken seriously as frightening beings who upset the natural order. How might they be performed today in order to convey a similar impression?

3 **hurlyburly**: confusion, i.e. the battle

5 **ere**: before

6 **heath**: open moorland

8–9 **Greymalkin ... Paddock**: names for a cat and a toad, animal shapes taken by the Witches' attendant spirits

10 **Anon**: We're coming at once

Scotland: open wasteland.

Thunder and lightning. Enter three Witches.

Witch 1	When shall we three meet again,
	In thunder, lightning or in rain?
Witch 2	When the hurlyburly's done,
	When the battle's lost and won.
Witch 3	That will be ere the set of sun.
Witch 1	Where the place?
Witch 2	Upon the heath.
Witch 3	There to meet with Macbeth.
Witch 1	I come, Greymalkin!
Witch 2	Paddock calls.
Witch 3	Anon!
All	Fair is foul, and foul is fair! –
	Hover through the fog and filthy air.

Witch 3 — That will be ere the set of sun.   5

Witch 3 — Anon!   10

Exeunt.

In this scene ...

- A soldier reports to King Duncan that the rebel Macdonwald and his Norwegian supporters have been defeated.
- He tells Duncan that the Scottish generals, Macbeth and Banquo, performed bravely in the battle.
- Duncan announces that he will sentence the rebel Thane of Cawdor to death and that Macbeth will be given his title.

King Duncan asks for a report of the battle between his forces and a rebel army. A wounded soldier tells Duncan that Macbeth has killed the rebel Macdonwald.

THINK ABOUT for GCSE

Language

- How would you describe the Captain's imagery? Think about how he conveys the ideas that (a) the battle was in the balance; (b) Macdonwald was wicked; and (c) luck, or fortune, is always changing sides.

2 **As ... plight**: judging by the bad state he's in

2–3 **revolt ... state**: latest developments in the rebellion

4 **hardy**: brave

5 **'Gainst my captivity**: to save me from being captured

6 **broil**: conflict

7 **Doubtful**: In the balance

8 **spent**: exhausted

9 **choke ... art**: block each other's efforts

10 **for to that**: i.e. to make him a rebel

11 **multiplying ... nature**: evil qualities

12–13 **from ... supplied**: is being helped by soldiers on foot and horse from Ireland and the Hebrides

14 **Fortune ... smiling**: the goddess of luck, favouring Macdonwald in his sinful cause

15 **Showed ... whore**: appeared like a prostitute, following the rebels

17 **Disdaining**: caring nothing for / scorning
    brandished steel: i.e. his drawn sword

19 **Valour's minion**: the special favourite of Courage

22 **unseamed ... chops**: tore him open from the stomach to the jaws

25–6 **whence ... break**: i.e. when fine spring weather often brings storms

Near Forres.

Drums beat a call to arms. Enter DUNCAN, *King of Scotland,
with* MALCOLM, DONALBAIN, LENNOX, *and soldiers.*

Enter (meeting them) a CAPTAIN, *bleeding from his wounds.*

DUNCAN	What bloody man is that? He can report,
	As seemeth by his plight, of the revolt
	The newest state.

MALCOLM	This is the sergeant	
	Who, like a good and hardy soldier, fought	
	'Gainst my captivity – Hail, brave friend!	5
	Say to the King the knowledge of the broil	
	As thou didst leave it.	

CAPTAIN	Doubtful it stood –	
	As two spent swimmers, that do cling together	
	And choke their art. The merciless Macdonwald	
	(Worthy to be a rebel, for to that	10
	The multiplying villainies of nature	
	Do swarm upon him) from the Western Isles	
	Of kerns and gallowglasses is supplied –	
	And Fortune, on his damnèd quarrel smiling,	
	Showed like a rebel's whore. But all's too weak –	15
	For brave Macbeth (well he deserves that name),	
	Disdaining Fortune, with his brandished steel	
	Which smoked with bloody execution,	
	Like Valour's minion, carved out his passage	
	Till he faced the slave –	20
	Which ne'er shook hands, nor bade farewell to him,	
	Till he unseamed him from the nave to the chops,	
	And fixed his head upon our battlements.	

DUNCAN	O valiant cousin! Worthy gentleman!

CAPTAIN	As whence the sun 'gins his reflection,	25
	Shipwrecking storms and direful thunders break –	
	So from that spring, whence comfort seemed to come,	

The soldier describes how Macbeth and Banquo then fought off an attack by the rebels' supporters, the invading Norwegians. Ross and Angus arrive with a further report of the battle.

30 **skipping**: lightly armed
  trust their heels: i.e. run away
31 **surveying vantage**: seeing his opportunity
32 **furbished arms**: fresh weapons

35 **As ... lion**: i.e. Macbeth and Banquo were no more frightened than fierce creatures would be of timid ones
36 **sooth**: truth
37 **over-charged ... cracks**: with double charges of gunpowder
39 **Except**: Unless
  reeking: i.e. steaming
40 **memorise another Golgotha**: make the battlefield as memorable as the scene of Christ's crucifixion
44 **smack**: are a sign

THINK ABOUT for GCSE

Characterisation

• What do we know about Macbeth so far? Think about how his physical courage and his capacity for violence are described.

Context

• Throughout Shakespeare's lifetime there had been a constant fear of invasion by Spain or other foreign countries. In what ways might this fear be reflected in this scene?

---

45 **Thane**: Scottish lord

46 **What ... eyes**: By the look of him, he's in a great hurry

50–1 **flout ... cold**: i.e. fly insultingly and put cold fear into our people
54 **dismal**: ominous (i.e. it looked as though it would end badly for the King's army)
55 **Bellona's ... proof**: Macbeth, heavily armoured, as though newly married to the goddess of war
56 **self-comparisons**: i.e. comparable skill and courage

	Discomfort swells. Mark, King of Scotland, mark!	
	No sooner justice had, with valour armed,	
	Compelled these skipping kerns to trust their heels,	30
	But the Norwegian lord, surveying vantage,	
	With furbished arms, and new supplies of men,	
	Began a fresh assault.	

DUNCAN   Dismayed not this
Our captains, Macbeth and Banquo?

CAPTAIN   Yes –
As sparrows eagles, or the hare the lion!   35
If I say sooth, I must report they were
As cannons over-charged with double cracks –
So they doubly redoubled strokes upon the foe.
Except they meant to bathe in reeking wounds,
Or memorise another Golgotha,   40
I cannot tell –
But I am faint. My gashes cry for help.

DUNCAN   So well thy words become thee, as thy wounds:
They smack of honour both. – Go, get him surgeons.

Exit CAPTAIN, *helped by soldiers.*

Enter ROSS *and* ANGUS.

Who comes here?

MALCOLM   The worthy Thane of Ross.   45

LENNOX   What a haste looks through his eyes!
So should he look that seems to speak things strange.

ROSS   God save the King!

DUNCAN   Whence cam'st thou, worthy thane?

ROSS   From Fife, great King –
Where the Norwegian banners flout the sky   50
And fan our people cold.
Norway himself, with terrible numbers,
Assisted by that most disloyal traitor,
The Thane of Cawdor, began a dismal conflict –
Till that Bellona's bridegroom, lapped in proof,   55
Confronted him with self-comparisons,

Ross reports that Macbeth has defeated the Norwegians. King Duncan orders that the rebel Thane of Cawdor shall be put to death and his title given to Macbeth.

58 **Curbing ... spirit**: i.e. disciplining Cawdor for daring to oppose the King

62 **craves composition**: is begging to discuss peace terms
63 **deign**: allow / grant
64 **disbursèd**: paid
    Inch: island

67 **our bosom interest**: matters close to our heart
    present: immediate

THINK ABOUT for GCSE

Themes and issues

• How does the account of Cawdor's actions and behaviour contribute to the theme of **deceit and equivocation**?

Language

• In what ways does the concluding line of this scene echo the concluding couplet of the first scene? What is the effect of that echo?

	Point against point, rebellious arm 'gainst arm,	
	Curbing his lavish spirit. And, to conclude,	
	The victory fell on us –	

DUNCAN   Great happiness!   60

ROSS   – That now
Sweno, the Norways' king, craves composition.
Nor would we deign him burial of his men
Till he disbursèd at Saint Colm's Inch
Ten thousand dollars to our general use.   65

DUNCAN   No more that Thane of Cawdor shall deceive
Our bosom interest! – Go, pronounce his present death,
And with his former title greet Macbeth.

ROSS   I'll see it done.

DUNCAN   What he hath lost, noble Macbeth hath won.   70

Exeunt.

In this scene ...

- Returning from the battle, Macbeth and Banquo meet the three Witches.
- They tell Macbeth that he will be Thane of Cawdor and King, and Banquo that he will be father to a line of kings, though never King himself.
- After the Witches have vanished, Ross and Angus arrive to tell Macbeth that he has been given the title Thane of Cawdor.
- Although Banquo warns him that Witches try to lure people to evil, Macbeth is excited by their prophecies.

The first Witch describes how she is going to torment a sailor whose wife has been rude to her.

2 **swine**: pigs

6 **quoth**: said
7 **Aroint thee**: Get out of here
   rump-fed ronyon: over-fed hag
9 **But ... sail**: People believed that witches could sail in sieves.
11 **I'll do**: i.e. I'll do him mischief

THINK ABOUT
for **GCSE**

Structure and form

- What does the Witches' proposed spell against the sailor tell us about how they might treat Macbeth?

Language

- How would you describe the rhythm and rhyme scheme of the Witch's curse (lines 15 to 26)? How does it fit what she is saying?

15 **have all the other**: i.e. have power over all the other winds
17–18 **quarters ... card**: compass-points on a sailor's chart

21 **penthouse lid**: eyelid
22 **forbid**: under a curse

24 **dwindle ... pine**: i.e. grow thinner and waste away
25 **bark**: ship

A heath.

Thunder.

***Enter three* WITCHES.**

WITCH 1	Where hast thou been, sister?
WITCH 2	Killing swine.
WITCH 3	Sister, where thou?

WITCH 1   A sailor's wife had chestnuts in her lap,
And munched, and munched, and munched.   **5**
'Give me,' quoth I.
'Aroint thee, witch!' the rump-fed ronyon cries.
Her husband's to Aleppo gone, master o' the *Tiger* –
But in a sieve I'll thither sail,
And like a rat without a tail,   **10**
I'll do, I'll do, and I'll do!

WITCH 2	I'll give thee a wind.
WITCH 1	Th' art kind.
WITCH 3	And I another.

WITCH 1   I myself have all the other –   **15**
And the very ports they blow,
All the quarters that they know
I' the shipman's card.
I'll drain him dry as hay!
Sleep shall neither night nor day   **20**
Hang upon his penthouse lid;
He shall live a man forbid.
Weary sev'n-nights nine times nine,
Shall he dwindle, peak and pine.
Though his bark cannot be lost,   **25**
Yet it shall be tempest-tossed!
Look what I have.

WITCH 2   Show me, show me.

Macbeth and Banquo see the Witches who greet Macbeth, addressing him as Thane of Glamis, Thane of Cawdor and King. Banquo asks them who they are.

29 **pilot**: sailor / navigator

33 **weird sisters**: sisters who share in the powers of fate, i.e. the Witches
34 **Posters**: fast travellers
36 **Thrice**: three times

38 **wound up**: completed

40 **is't called**: is it supposed to be

41 **attire**: clothing

43 **aught**: the kind of creatures

45 **choppy**: chapped / with cracked skin

THINK ABOUT for GCSE

Structure and form

• What do you think the Witches' 'charm' (line 38) may be intended to do?

Performance and staging

• What clues are there in Banquo's speech (lines 52 to 58) to indicate how Macbeth should be reacting at this point?

51 **hereafter**: at some time in the future

54 **fantastical**: imaginary
56 **present grace**: his current title (i.e. Thane of Glamis)
57 **Of noble ... hope**: i.e. as a man who will achieve even greater fortune and the chance of being King
58 **rapt withal**: completely carried away / in a trance

| WITCH 1 | Here I have a pilot's thumb, |
| | Wrecked, as homeward he did come. | 30 |

Drum beats in the distance.

| WITCH 3 | A drum! A drum! |
| | Macbeth doth come. |

ALL	The weird sisters, hand in hand,
	Posters of the sea and land,
	Thus do go about, about –	35
	Thrice to thine, and thrice to mine,
	And thrice again, to make up nine.
	Peace! – the charm's wound up.

Enter MACBETH and BANQUO.

| MACBETH | So foul and fair a day I have not seen. |

BANQUO	How far is't called to Forres? –
	(*seeing the* WITCHES) What are these,	40
	So withered and so wild in their attire? –
	That look not like th' inhabitants o' the earth
	And yet are on't? – Live you? Or are you aught
	That man may question? You seem to understand me,
	By each at once her choppy finger laying	45
	Upon her skinny lips. You should be women,
	And yet your beards forbid me to interpret
	That you are so.

| MACBETH | Speak, if you can! – What are you? |

| WITCH 1 | All hail, Macbeth! Hail to thee, Thane of Glamis! |

| WITCH 2 | All hail, Macbeth! Hail to thee, Thane of Cawdor! | 50 |

| WITCH 3 | All hail, Macbeth – that shalt be King hereafter! |

BANQUO	Good sir, why do you start and seem to fear
	Things that do sound so fair? (*To the* WITCHES) I' the
	name of truth,
	Are ye fantastical, or that indeed
	Which outwardly ye show? My noble partner	55
	You greet with present grace, and great prediction
	Of noble having and of royal hope,
	That he seems rapt withal. To me you speak not.

Banquo asks the Witches to predict his future. They tell him that his descendants will be kings, though he himself will not. Macbeth tries to question the Witches, but they vanish.

THINK ABOUT for GCSE

Structure and form

- What do you notice about the different ways in which the Witches greet Macbeth and Banquo? How might we account for the difference?

Performance and staging

- How could the Witches 'vanish' (line 79) in a performance? Think how they might be made to vanish in: (a) a school hall; (b) a modern theatre; (c) Shakespeare's Globe; and (d) a film.

Themes and issues

- The Witches' prophecies (lines 49 to 68) offer Macbeth and Banquo only partial truths; in their ambiguous pronouncements they are deliberately **equivocating**. What messages might Macbeth and Banquo take away from this meeting, and in what ways might they be **deceived**?

59 **look … time**: i.e. predict the future

68 **get**: be the father of
   be none: will not be one

71 **imperfect**: unfinished, i.e. they tell only part of the story
72 **Sinel**: Macbeth's father
74 **prosperous**: successful and wealthy
75–6 **Stands not … more**: is no more believable

78 **blasted**: windswept
79 **charge**: order

82 **corporal**: flesh and blood
83 **Would**: I wish

85–6 **the insane … prisoner**: hemlock, or similar plant, which drives people mad

	If you can look into the seeds of time,	
	And say which grain will grow, and which will not,	60
	Speak then to me, who neither beg nor fear	
	Your favours nor your hate.	

WITCH 1   Hail!

WITCH 2   Hail!

WITCH 3   Hail!   65

WITCH 1   Lesser than Macbeth, and greater.

WITCH 2   Not so happy, yet much happier.

WITCH 3   Thou shalt get kings, though thou be none.
So all hail, Macbeth and Banquo!

WITCH 1   Banquo and Macbeth, all hail!   70

MACBETH   Stay, you imperfect speakers! Tell me more.
By Sinel's death, I know I am Thane of Glamis –
But how of Cawdor? The Thane of Cawdor lives,
A prosperous gentleman – and to be King
Stands not within the prospect of belief   75
No more than to be Cawdor. Say, from whence
You owe this strange intelligence? Or why
Upon this blasted heath you stop our way
With such prophetic greeting? Speak, I charge you!

The WITCHES *vanish.*

BANQUO   The earth hath bubbles, as the water has,   80
And these are of them. – Whither are they vanished?

MACBETH   Into the air – and what seemed corporal, melted
As breath into the wind. – Would they had stayed!

BANQUO   Were such things here, as we do speak about?
– Or have we eaten on the insane root   85
That takes the reason prisoner?

MACBETH   Your children shall be kings.

BANQUO   *You* shall be King.

MACBETH   And Thane of Cawdor too – went it not so?

Ross and Angus arrive to give Macbeth some news. As a reward for having defeated the rebels, King Duncan is giving him the title Thane of Cawdor. Angus explains that the existing Thane of Cawdor was a traitor and is due to be executed.

92 **venture**: daring

93–4 **His wonders ... his**: i.e. he does not know whether to praise you or express his amazement

96 **stout**: brave

97 **Nothing afeard**: completely unafraid

99 **post with post**: one messenger after another

103 **herald ... sight**: lead you to his presence

105 **for an earnest**: as a promise

107 **addition**: title

THINK ABOUT for GCSE

Characterisation

• What does the news that Ross brings (lines 90 to 108) show about Duncan's opinion of Macbeth? What effect do you think it might have on Macbeth at this point, bearing in mind the Witches' prophecies?

• Look at Macbeth's aside (lines 117 to 118). What is going through his head that he is not willing to share with the others?

110 **Who *was***: The man who used to be
     yet: still

112 **combined**: allied, i.e. fighting on the same side as

113 **line**: strengthen

114 **vantage**: advantages

115 **wreck**: ruin

116 **capital**: carrying the death penalty

118 **behind**: yet to come

Banquo	To the selfsame tune and words. Who's here?

Enter Ross *and* Angus.

Ross	The King hath happily received, Macbeth,	90
	The news of thy success. And, when he reads	
	Thy personal venture in the rebels' fight,	
	His wonders and his praises do contend,	
	Which should be thine, or his. Silenced with that,	
	In viewing o'er the rest o' the selfsame day,	95
	He finds thee in the stout Norwegian ranks,	
	Nothing afeard of what thyself didst make,	
	Strange images of death. As thick as hail	
	Ran post with post – and every one did bear	
	Thy praises in his kingdom's great defence,	100
	And poured them down before him.	

Angus	We are sent
	To give thee, from our royal master, thanks –
	Only to herald thee into his sight,
	Not pay thee.

Ross	And, for an earnest of a greater honour,	105
	He bade me, from him, call thee Thane of Cawdor:	
	In which addition, hail, most worthy thane! –	
	For it is thine.	

Banquo	What! Can the devil speak true?

Macbeth	The Thane of Cawdor lives. Why do you dress me
	In borrowed robes?

Angus	Who *was* the thane lives yet –	110
	But under heavy judgement bears that life	
	Which he deserves to lose. Whether he was combined	
	With those of Norway, or did line the rebel	
	With hidden help and vantage, or that with both	
	He laboured in his country's wreck, I know not.	115
	But treasons capital, confessed and proved,	
	Have overthrown him.	

Macbeth	(*Aside*) Glamis, and Thane of Cawdor!
	The greatest is behind. (*To* Ross *and* Angus) Thanks
	for your pains.

Macbeth is amazed that the Witches' prediction has come true. Banquo warns him that the Witches might be leading him to evil, but Macbeth begins to think about murdering King Duncan.

121–2 **That … crown**: If you believed that, it might encourage your hopes of becoming King

124 **win … harm**: lead us to destruction

125 **instruments of darkness**: agents of evil

126 **honest trifles**: unimportant truths

127 **deepest consequence**: things that really matter

129 **happy prologues**: promising introductions
swelling: impressive / ascending

130 **imperial theme**: story or topic of being a king

131 **soliciting**: temptation

133 **earnest**: promise

136 **unfix my hair**: make my hair stand on end

137 **seated**: i.e. fixed in place

140 **but fantastical**: only in my imagination

141 **Shakes … man**: disturbs my being

141–2 **function … surmise**: imagination and doubt make me incapable of action

143 **rapt**: lost in thought / in a trance

145 **Without my stir**: without my doing anything

146 **our … mould**: new clothes, which do not fit properly

147–8 **Come … day**: Whatever will happen, will happen, as nothing stops the passage of time

THINK ABOUT for GCSE

Language

• What does the language of lines 128 to 143 tell us about Macbeth's state of mind?

Themes and issues

• What do the following lines have in common: 66, 67, 68, 82, 85 to 86, 132, and 142 to 143? How do they add to the feeling that the **natural order** of things seems turned upside-down in this play?

	(*To* BANQUO) Do you not hope your children shall be kings,
	When those that gave the Thane of Cawdor to me
	Promised no less to them?

BANQUO   That, trusted home,
Might yet enkindle you unto the crown
Besides the Thane of Cawdor. But 'tis strange –
And oftentimes, to win us to our harm,
The instruments of darkness tell us truths,   125
Win us with honest trifles, to betray 's
In deepest consequence. –
(*To* Ross *and* ANGUS) Cousins, a word, I pray you.

MACBETH   (*Aside*) Two truths are told
As happy prologues to the swelling act
Of the imperial theme. (*To* Ross *and* ANGUS) I thank
   you, gentlemen.   130
(*Aside*) This supernatural soliciting
Cannot be ill – cannot be good. If ill,
Why hath it given me earnest of success,
Commencing in a truth? I am Thane of Cawdor.
If good, why do I yield to that suggestion   135
Whose horrid image doth unfix my hair,
And make my seated heart knock at my ribs
Against the use of nature? Present fears
Are less than horrible imaginings.
My thought, whose murder yet is but fantastical,   140
Shakes so my single state of man, that function
Is smothered in surmise, and nothing is
But what is not.

BANQUO   (*To* Ross *and* ANGUS) Look how our partner's rapt.

MACBETH   (*Aside*) If chance will have me king, why, chance
   may crown me,
Without my stir.

BANQUO   New honours come upon him   145
Like our strange garments – cleave not to their mould
But with the aid of use.

MACBETH   (*Aside*) Come what come may,
Time and the hour runs through the roughest day.

Macbeth hides his thoughts and
they all depart to meet King
Duncan.

149 **stay … leisure**: are ready to leave
when it suits you
150 **favour**: pardon
150–1 **wrought … forgotten**: troubled by past
events
151–3 **your pains … them**: i.e. every day I
am reminded of what you have done
for me
154 **chanced**: happened
155 **The interim … it**: after we have
thought it over in the meantime

THINK ABOUT
for GCSE

Characterisation

• What is your impression of
Banquo so far? Think about,
for example, what his
comment to Macbeth (lines
121 to 127) suggests about
him, and his attitude to the
Witches (line 108).

28

BANQUO	Worthy Macbeth, we stay upon your leisure.

MACBETH   Give me your favour. My dull brain was wrought   150
With things forgotten. Kind gentlemen, your pains
Are registered where every day I turn
The leaf to read them. – Let us toward the king. –
(*To* BANQUO) Think upon what hath chanced – and at
   more time,
The interim having weighed it, let us speak   155
Our free hearts each to other.

BANQUO   Very gladly.

MACBETH   Till then, enough. – Come, friends.

Exeunt.

In this scene ...

- Duncan thanks Macbeth and Banquo for the part they played in defeating the rebels.
- Macbeth's secret hope to become King receives a setback when Duncan announces that his eldest son, Malcolm, will be the heir to the throne.

King Duncan's son, Malcolm, reports that the rebel Thane of Cawdor faced his execution with dignity. Duncan thanks Macbeth and Banquo for the parts they played in the battle. Macbeth expresses his loyalty to Duncan.

THINK ABOUT *for* GCSE

Structure and form

- A situation in which the audience knows something important that a character does not is described as 'dramatic irony'. Looking at lines 11 to 14, think about the dramatic irony in (a) the comment being made by Duncan at the very moment Macbeth enters; and (b) the term used by Duncan to greet Macbeth.

2 **in commission**: who were given the responsibility (of executing Cawdor)
liege: lord / sovereign

6 **set forth**: displayed

8 **Became ... it**: showed his good qualities as much as the way he died
9 **been ... death**: practised his preparation for death
10 **owed**: owned
11 **As ... trifle**: as though it were something of no value
art: skill
12 **the mind's construction**: i.e. what someone thinks and feels

15 **sin ... ingratitude**: Duncan feels that he has done wrong in not yet rewarding Macbeth.
16–18 **Thou ... thee**: i.e. Macbeth has performed so well that Duncan cannot keep up with the rewards he owes him
18 **Would**: I wish
19–20 **That ... mine**: so that I would have been able to reward you as much as your merits deserve
21 **More is thy due**: you are owed more
23 **pays itself**: is its own reward
26 **but**: only
26–7 **doing ... toward**: protecting

Forres: the palace.

Trumpet fanfare. Enter King Duncan, *with* Malcolm, Donalbain, Lennox, *and attendants.*

Duncan	Is execution done on Cawdor? Or not
	Those in commission yet returned?

Malcolm   My liege,
They are not yet come back. But I have spoke
With one that saw him die: who did report
That very frankly he confessed his treasons,   5
Implored your Highness' pardon, and set forth
A deep repentance. Nothing in his life
Became him like the leaving it. He died
As one that had been studied in his death,
To throw away the dearest thing he owed   10
As 'twere a careless trifle.

Duncan   There's no art
To find the mind's construction in the face.
He was a gentleman on whom I built
An absolute trust –

Enter Macbeth, Banquo, Ross, *and* Angus.

(*To* Macbeth) O worthiest cousin!
The sin of my ingratitude even now   15
Was heavy on me. Thou art so far before,
That swiftest wing of recompense is slow
To overtake thee. Would thou hadst less deserved,
That the proportion both of thanks and payment
Might have been mine! Only I have left to say,   20
More is thy due than more than all can pay.

Macbeth   The service and the loyalty I owe,
In doing it, pays itself. Your Highness' part
Is to receive our duties. And our duties
Are to your throne and state, children and servants –   25
Which do but what they should, by doing everything
Safe toward your love and honour.

Macbeth is unsettled when Duncan announces that his eldest son, Malcolm, will succeed him as King. Malcolm is an obstacle to Macbeth's ambitions, which will have to be overcome.

THINK ABOUT for GCSE

Characterisation

• What does Macbeth's aside (lines 48 to 53) suggest about the way his mind is working at this point? Think about what he means by 'o'erleap' and what his 'black and deep desires' might be.

Language

• What image is used in lines 28 to 33? What does Banquo's reply (lines 32 to 33) suggest about a king's relationship to his subjects?

31   **enfold**: embrace

33–5   **My plenteous ... sorrow**: i.e. I am so overcome with joy that I am weeping

36   **nearest**: closest in line to the throne
37–8   **establish ... eldest**: settle who will succeed to the throne by naming our eldest son
39   **Prince of Cumberland**: the title held by the heir to the Scottish throne
39–40   **which ... only**: i.e. the title for Malcolm will not be the only honour handed out
41–2   **signs ... deservers**: everybody who deserves an honour will receive one
43   **bind us further**: increase our debt / bond us
44   **The rest ... you**: Anything not done on your behalf is hard work
harbinger: officer sent ahead to make arrangements

52   **The eye ... hand**: Let my eyes not see what my hand is doing

DUNCAN	Welcome hither!
	I have begun to plant thee, and will labour
	To make thee full of growing. – Noble Banquo,
	That hast no less deserved, nor must be known **30**
	No less to have done so – let me enfold thee,
	And hold thee to my heart.
BANQUO	There if I grow,
	The harvest is your own.
DUNCAN	My plenteous joys,
	Wanton in fulness, seek to hide themselves
	In drops of sorrow. – Sons, kinsmen, thanes, **35**
	And you whose places are the nearest, know:
	We will establish our estate upon
	Our eldest, Malcolm; whom we name hereafter
	The Prince of Cumberland – which honour must
	Not unaccompanied invest him only, **40**
	But signs of nobleness, like stars, shall shine
	On all deservers. – (*To* MACBETH) From hence to
	Inverness,
	And bind us further to you.
MACBETH	The rest is labour, which is not used for you.
	I'll be myself the harbinger, and make joyful **45**
	The hearing of my wife with your approach. –
	So, humbly take my leave.
DUNCAN	My worthy Cawdor!
MACBETH	(*Aside*) The Prince of Cumberland! – That is a step
	On which I must fall down, or else o'erleap,
	For in my way it lies. Stars, hide your fires! **50**
	Let not light see my black and deep desires! –
	The eye wink at the hand! – Yet let that be,
	Which the eye fears, when it is done, to see.

Exit.

Duncan leads his lords away, still praising Macbeth.

54 **full so**: so very
55 **in ... fed**: it is food to me to hear him praised

58 **peerless**: without a rival (i.e. there is no-one to compare with him)

THINK ABOUT *for* **GCSE**

Themes and issues

• **Kingship**: In your opinion, what kind of king does Duncan appear to be from these early scenes? Think about how he treats his followers and what they seem to think of him.

DUNCAN   True, worthy Banquo: he is full so valiant,
               And in his commendations I am fed –   55
               It is a banquet to me. Let's after him,
               Whose care is gone before to bid us welcome.
               It is a peerless kinsman.

                                    Trumpets sound. Exeunt.

In this scene ...

- Lady Macbeth receives a letter from her husband in which he tells her about his meeting with the Witches.
- She fears that he is too good-natured to kill Duncan, and decides to use all her powers to persuade him.
- Receiving news that Duncan plans to spend that night at their castle, she calls upon evil spirits to toughen her for the murder.
- Lady Macbeth advises Macbeth to leave everything to her.

Lady Macbeth reads a letter from Macbeth telling her about the Witches' prophecy that he is Thane of Cawdor and will be King. She worries that her husband has too much natural goodness in him to kill Duncan.

THINK ABOUT for GCSE

Relationships

- What do we learn about Macbeth from his letter to his wife? Has he ever talked to his wife about becoming King, do you think? Has he already decided to kill Duncan? What is his attitude to the Witches?

- What does Lady Macbeth fear about her husband's character? Do you think that fear is justified, from what you have seen so far?

2 **perfectest**: most reliable

5 **rapt ... wonder**: lost in amazement
6 **missives**: messengers

8–9 **coming on of time**: future
10 **deliver thee**: report to you

11 **dues of rejoicing**: i.e. excitement of knowing what great things are in store for you

16 **milk ... kindness**: natural human goodness

17 **catch ... way**: take the quickest route
wouldst: would like to

19 **illness**: wickedness / ruthlessness
attend: accompany

19–20 **What ... holily**: i.e. Anything you really want, you want to get by fair means

20 **wouldst ... false**: you don't want to cheat

21 **wouldst ... win**: you are happy to win unfairly

21–4 **Thou'dst ... undone**: i.e. While you want the murder done, you're afraid to do it yourself

24 **Hie thee hither**: Hurry here

25 **That I ... ear**: So that I can influence you with courage and ruthlessness

26–7 **chastise ... round**: beat down with my arguments everything that stands between you and the crown

28 **metaphysical aid**: supernatural help

29 **tidings**: news

ACT 1   SCENE 5

Inverness: inside Macbeth's castle.

Enter LADY MACBETH, *with a letter.*

LADY MACBETH (*Reading*) 'They met me in the day of success – and I
have learned by the perfectest report, they have more in
them than mortal knowledge. When I burned in desire
to question them further, they made themselves air, into
which they vanished. Whiles I stood rapt in the wonder   5
of it, came missives from the King, who all-hailed me
Thane of Cawdor – by which title, before, these weird
sisters saluted me; and referred me to the coming on of
time, with "Hail, King that shalt be!" This have I thought
good to deliver thee, my dearest partner of greatness,   10
that thou might'st not lose the dues of rejoicing by being
ignorant of what greatness is promised thee. Lay it to thy
heart, and farewell.'

Glamis thou art, and Cawdor – and shalt be
What thou art promised! – Yet do I fear thy nature.   15
It is too full o' the milk of human kindness
To catch the nearest way. Thou wouldst be great –
Art not without ambition, but without
The illness should attend it. What thou wouldst highly,
That wouldst thou holily – wouldst not play false,   20
And yet wouldst wrongly win. Thou'dst have, great
     Glamis,
That which cries 'Thus thou must do, if thou have it' –
And that which rather thou dost fear to do,
Than wishest should be undone. Hie thee hither! –
That I may pour my spirits in thine ear,   25
And chastise with the valour of my tongue
All that impedes thee from the golden round,
Which fate and metaphysical aid doth seem
To have thee crowned withal. –

Enter a MESSENGER.

                    What is your tidings?

Lady Macbeth is excited to hear that King Duncan is coming to stay in their castle that very night. Just as she is calling upon evil spirits to assist her in helping Macbeth to kill Duncan, Macbeth arrives.

THINK ABOUT for GCSE

Characterisation

- Which phrases in Lady Macbeth's two soliloquies (speeches in which a character says his or her thoughts aloud), in lines 14 to 29, and 37 to 53, suggest that she has already decided that they have to kill Duncan?

Language

- Find the examples of language to do with darkness and night in lines 36 to 53, and in Macbeth's speech in Act 1 Scene 4, lines 48 to 53. What does it tell us about the Macbeths? In what ways are they involving the natural world in their plots?

32 **informed for preparation**: told me to get things ready

34 **had the speed of**: overtook

36 **Give him tending**: Look after him
37 **raven**: Ravens were thought to be messengers of death.

39–40 **spirits ... on**: evil spirits who listen to
40 **mortal thoughts**: murderous plans
     unsex me: take away my female qualities

44 **That ... nature**: so that no pangs of conscience
45 **fell**: deadly
46 **Th' effect and it**: my plan and the achievement of it
47 **take ... gall**: exchange my milk for bitter poison
     ministers: agents (of evil)
48 **sightless substances**: invisible bodies
49 **wait ... mischief**: serve the evil in nature
50 **pall ... dunnest**: cover / shroud yourself in the darkest
53 **Hold**: Stop

56 **ignorant present**: i.e. not knowing what will happen in the future
57 **the instant**: what is happening now

59 **as he purposes**: so he intends

MESSENGER	The King comes here tonight.

LADY MACBETH   Thou'rt mad to say it!   30
Is not thy master with him? – Who, were't so,
Would have informed for preparation.

MESSENGER   So please you, it is true: our Thane is coming.
One of my fellows had the speed of him –
Who, almost dead for breath, had scarcely more   35
Than would make up his message.

LADY MACBETH   Give him tending:
He brings great news. (***Exit** MESSENGER.*) The raven
      himself is hoarse
That croaks the fatal entrance of Duncan
Under my battlements. Come, you spirits
That tend on mortal thoughts, unsex me here! –   40
And fill me, from the crown to the toe, top-full
Of direst cruelty! Make thick my blood,   *consonance*
Stop up th' access and passage to remorse –   *unpleasant*
                                                              et noise
That no compunctious visitings of nature
Shake my fell purpose, nor keep peace between   45
Th' effect and it! Come to my woman's breasts,
And take my milk for gall, you murdering ministers,
Wherever in your sightless substances
You wait on nature's mischief! Come, thick night,
And pall thee in the dunnest smoke of hell –   50
That my keen knife see not the wound it makes,
Nor heaven peep through the blanket of the dark
To cry, "Hold, hold!"

Enter MACBETH.

                                              Great Glamis! Worthy Cawdor!
Greater than both, by the all-hail hereafter!
Thy letters have transported me beyond   55
This ignorant present, and I feel now
The future in the instant.

MACBETH   My dearest love,
Duncan comes here tonight.

LADY MACBETH   And when goes hence?

MACBETH   Tomorrow, as he purposes.

Determined to go through with the murder of Duncan, Lady Macbeth tells Macbeth to look innocent and leave everything to her.

62–3 To ... time: To deceive people, look as they expect you to look at the time

66 provided for: 1 looked after; 2 dealt with

67 dispatch: management

69 solely ... sway: absolute power of being King

70 Only ... clear: Just appear innocent

71 To alter ... fear: Changing your expression is always a sign of fear

THINK ABOUT for GCSE

Themes and issues

- **Deceit and equivocation** is a major theme in this play. What do the two images in lines 61 to 65 mean? What advice is Lady Macbeth giving her husband?

Characterisation

- What else do Lady Macbeth's speeches reveal about the kind of person she is and the kind of relationship she has with Macbeth?

LADY MACBETH	O! – never
	Shall sun that morrow see!
	Your face, my thane, is as a book, where men
	May read strange matters. To beguile the time,
	Look like the time. Bear welcome in your eye,
	Your hand, your tongue: look like the innocent flower
	But be the serpent under 't. He that's coming
	Must be provided for. And you shall put
	This night's great business into my dispatch –
	Which shall to all our nights and days to come
	Give solely sovereign sway and masterdom.
MACBETH	We will speak further.
LADY MACBETH	Only look up clear.
	To alter favour ever is to fear.
	Leave all the rest to me.

60

65

70

Exeunt.

In this scene ...
- King Duncan arrives at the Macbeths' castle.
- Lady Macbeth welcomes him.

King Duncan arrives at the Macbeths' castle with Banquo and other lords. He admires the castle's beautiful setting and is welcomed by Lady Macbeth.

THINK ABOUT
for GCSE

Themes and issues

- **Deceit and equivocation:** What is there about the characters' comments in lines 1 to 10 that might cause us to recall the Witches' line 'Fair is foul, and foul is fair' (Act 1 Scene 1, line 11)?

Structure and form

- How is dramatic irony (see page 30) used in ths short scene?

1 **seat**: situation
2 **Nimbly ... itself**: eagerly shows its sweet qualities

4 **temple-haunting martlet**: house-martin which builds its nest on church walls
   approve: prove
5 **loved mansionry**: favourite home
6 **wooingly**: appealingly
6–7 **jutty ... Buttress**: parts of the stonework that stick out
7 **coign of vantage**: convenient corner
8 **pendent ... cradle**: hanging nest and cradle for its young

11 **our trouble**: a trouble to us
12 **still**: always
13 **yield**: reward

16 **single**: simple
16–17 **contend Against**: i.e. try to match
18 **of old**: in the past
19 **late ... up**: honours added recently
20 **rest your hermits**: will always pray for you, as hermits do

Inverness: the approach to Macbeth's castle.

Musicians play a welcoming fanfare (oboes). Torches burn to light the entrance of the castle.

Enter King Duncan, *with* Malcolm, Donalbain, Banquo, Lennox, Macduff, Ross, Angus, *and attendants.*

DUNCAN   This castle hath a pleasant seat. The air
Nimbly and sweetly recommends itself
Unto our gentle senses.

BANQUO   This guest of summer,
The temple-haunting martlet, does approve,
By his loved mansionry, that the heaven's breath   5
Smells wooingly here. No jutty, frieze,
Buttress, nor coign of vantage, but this bird
Hath made his pendent bed and procreant cradle.
Where they most breed and haunt, I have observed,
The air is delicate.

Enter Lady Macbeth.

DUNCAN   See, see – our honoured hostess!   10
(*To* Lady Macbeth) The love that follows us sometime
    is our trouble,
Which still we thank as love. Herein I teach you,
How you shall bid God yield us for your pains,
And thank us for your trouble.

LADY MACBETH   All our service,
In every point twice done, and then done double,   15
Were poor and single business, to contend
Against those honours deep and broad wherewith
Your Majesty loads our house. For those of old,
And the late dignities heaped up to them,
We rest your hermits.

Lady Macbeth welcomes Duncan, and then takes him to meet Macbeth.

21 **coursed … heels**: chased closely behind him
22 **purveyor**: official who rode ahead of the King
23 **holp**: helped

26 **in count**: in trust / account
27 **make their audit**: present their financial report
28 **Still**: always

31 **By your leave**: With your permission

THINK ABOUT for GCSE

Language

• In Lady Macbeth's reply (lines 25 to 28) 'count' means 'account', and 'audit' is a 'financial report'. What point is she getting across with this financial imagery?

Themes and issues

• **Deceit and equivocation**: How would you describe Lady Macbeth's welcome of Duncan? Which image from the previous scene might we recall when we hear her words to him?

DUNCAN   Where's the Thane of Cawdor?   **20**
We coursed him at the heels, and had a purpose
To be his purveyor. But he rides well –
And his great love, sharp as his spur, hath holp him
To his home before us. Fair and noble hostess,
We are your guest tonight.

LADY MACBETH   Your servants ever   **25**
Have theirs, themselves, and what is theirs in count
To make their audit at your Highness' pleasure –
Still to return your own.

DUNCAN   Give me your hand.
Conduct me to mine host. We love him highly,
And shall continue our graces towards him.   **30**
By your leave, hostess.

Exeunt.

In this scene ...

- Macbeth has left the banquet, tormented by doubts about murdering Duncan.
- When Lady Macbeth comes to fetch him back in to the banquet, he declares that they must not go ahead with the murder.
- Lady Macbeth explains how the blame for the murder can be laid upon Duncan's attendants. She persuades Macbeth to go ahead with the plan.

Macbeth is deeply troubled by what might happen if he kills King Duncan. He considers Duncan's virtues and the powerful reasons for not committing the crime.

THINK ABOUT for GCSE

Characterisation

- What does Macbeth's soliloquy reveal about his attitude to killing Duncan? It might help to consider the speech in three sections: lines 1 to 7, 7 to 12, and 12 to 28.

Themes and issues

- **Kingship**: In what ways does this speech help us to understand how terrible it is to kill a king, especially a king like Duncan?

---

s.d. **Sewer**: person in charge of servants

1 **If ... done**: i.e. If the killing could be the end of the business

3–4 **trammel ... success**: i.e. prevent any further trouble and achieve success with Duncan's death

5 **the be-all ... here**: the end of the business here on earth

6 **bank ... time**: i.e. this narrow island of life (compared with eternity)

7 **jump ... come**: i.e. risk punishment in the after-life

8 **still ... here**: always receive justice here on earth

8–10 **that ... inventor**: because we give lessons in violence which are then used against us

11–12 **Commends ... lips**: makes us drink our own poison

12 **He's ... trust**: There are two reasons why Duncan should be able to trust me

17 **borne ... meek**: used his power so gently

18 **clear ... office**: free from guilt as a king

20 **taking-off**: murder

22 **Striding the blast**: i.e. joining the storm of horror at the murder
cherubin: angel

23 **sightless couriers**: invisible runners (i.e. the winds)

25–6 **no spur ... intent**: i.e. nothing to drive my intention forward

27–8 **o'erleaps ... other**: jumps too high and falls on the other side

Inverness: inside the castle.

Torch-light. Music is heard from the great hall. A Sewer leads a line of servants past with dishes for a banquet.

Then enter MACBETH, *alone.*

MACBETH   If it were done when 'tis done, then 'twere well
             It were done quickly. If th' assassination
             Could trammel up the consequence, and catch
             With his surcease success – that but this blow
             Might be the be-all and the end-all here,   5
             But here, upon this bank and shoal of time,
             We'd jump the life to come. – But in these cases
             We still have judgement here – that we but teach
             Bloody instructions, which, being taught, return
             To plague th' inventor. This even-handed justice   10
             Commends th' ingredients of our poisoned chalice
             To our own lips. He's here in double trust:
             First, as I am his kinsman and his subject,
             Strong both against the deed – then, as his host,
             Who should against his murderer shut the door,   15
             Not bear the knife myself! Besides, this Duncan
             Hath borne his faculties so meek, hath been
             So clear in his great office, that his virtues
             Will plead like angels, trumpet-tongued, against
             The deep damnation of his taking-off.   20
             And pity, like a naked new-born babe,
             Striding the blast, or heaven's cherubin, horsed
             Upon the sightless couriers of the air,
             Shall blow the horrid deed in every eye,
             That tears shall drown the wind! – I have no spur   25
             To prick the sides of my intent, but only
             Vaulting ambition, which o'erleaps itself
             And falls on the other –

Enter LADY MACBETH.

                               How now? What news?

When Macbeth tells his wife that they must not go ahead with their plan, she accuses him of being a coward. She declares that she would rather kill her own baby than break a promise like this as Macbeth has done.

THINK ABOUT for GCSE

Relationships

• What methods does Lady Macbeth use to persuade her husband to kill Duncan? Think about what arguments she employs in lines 35 to 39, 39 to 45, 49, and 54 to 59. What does this approach suggest about their relationship?

Themes and issues

• **Manhood**: How would you describe the language Lady Macbeth uses to persuade her husband? What do Lady Macbeth's speeches reveal about her view of what a 'real man' is? Look at line 49, for example.

29 **supped**: i.e. finished his meal

32–3 **bought ... opinions**: earned a fine reputation
34 **worn ... gloss**: i.e. enjoyed while they are still new to me

35–6 **Was ... yourself**: Was your earlier ambition as shaky as a drunken man
37 **green and pale**: sick (with a hangover)

39 **account**: regard / consider
40–1 **be the ... desire**: match your desires with deeds
42 **esteem'st**: value as
ornament of life: i.e. the crown
44 **Letting ... would**: not daring to do what you want to do
45 **adage**: proverb
Prithee: I beg you
46 **may become**: is fitting for
47 **none**: i.e. not human

48 **break**: reveal

50 **more ... were**: i.e. to be king
51–2 **Nor ... both**: Neither the time nor the place were right then, but you were prepared to make them right
53–4 **They ... you**: Now that the circumstances are right, that has made you lose your courage
54 **given suck**: fed a baby with my own milk

LADY MACBETH	He has almost supped. Why have you left the chamber?
MACBETH	Hath he asked for me?
LADY MACBETH	Know you not he has? 30

MACBETH   We will proceed no further in this business.
He hath honoured me of late – and I have bought
Golden opinions from all sorts of people,
Which would be worn now in their newest gloss,
Not cast aside so soon.

LADY MACBETH   Was the hope drunk, 35
Wherein you dressed yourself? Hath it slept since?
And wakes it now to look so green and pale
At what it did so freely? From this time
Such I account thy love. Art thou afeard
To be the same in thine own act and valour, 40
As thou art in desire? Wouldst thou have that
Which thou esteem'st the ornament of life,
And live a coward in thine own esteem,
Letting 'I dare not' wait upon 'I would,'
Like the poor cat i'the adage?

MACBETH   Prithee, peace. 45
I dare do all that may become a man –
Who dares do more is none.

LADY MACBETH   What beast was't then
That made you break this enterprise to me?
When you durst do it, then you were a man!
And, to be more than what you were, you would 50
Be so much more the man. Nor time nor place
Did then adhere, and yet you would make both.
They have made themselves, and that their fitness now
Does unmake you. I have given suck, and know
How tender 'tis to love the babe that milks me. 55
I would, while it was smiling in my face,
Have plucked my nipple from his boneless gums,
And dashed the brains out! – had I so sworn as you
Have done to this.

MACBETH   If we should fail, –

Lady Macbeth explains to Macbeth her plan to blame the murder of Duncan on his attendants. Persuaded by his wife, Macbeth agrees to go through with the murder.

60   **But ... sticking-place**: i.e. just keep your nerve

62–3   **Whereto ... him**: and he is all the more likely to sleep deeply after his hard journey

63   **chamberlains**: attendants in his bed-chamber

64   **with ... convince**: overpower with wine and strong drink

65   **warder**: guardian

66   **a fume**: i.e. foggy
receipt of reason: i.e. the brain

67   **limbeck**: flask for impure liquids
swinish: pig-like

70   **put upon**: blame on

71   **spongy**: drink-sodden

72   **quell**: murder

73   **undaunted mettle**: fearless spirit

74   **received**: believed / accepted as the truth

77   **other**: in any other way

78   **As ... roar**: because we will loudly express our grief and fury

79   **I am settled**: i.e. My mind is made up
bend up: summon up

80   **Each corporal agent**: all the powers of my body

81   **mock ... show**: deceive everybody

THINK ABOUT for GCSE

Characterisation

- At the end of Act 1 Scene 5 Lady Macbeth said, 'Leave all the rest to me'. In what ways has she been true to her word in this scene?

- What do you make of Macbeth's reactions to his wife's arguments? What is his view now of what they have to do?

LADY MACBETH	We fail?
	But screw your courage to the sticking-place 60
	And we'll not fail! When Duncan is asleep
	(Whereto the rather shall his day's hard journey
	Soundly invite him), his two chamberlains
	Will I with wine and wassail so convince,
	That memory, the warder of the brain, 65
	Shall be a fume, and the receipt of reason
	A limbeck only. When in swinish sleep
	Their drenchèd natures lie, as in a death,
	What cannot you and I perform upon
	Th' unguarded Duncan? What not put upon 70
	His spongy officers, who shall bear the guilt
	Of our great quell?
MACBETH	Bring forth men-children only! –
	For thy undaunted mettle should compose
	Nothing but males. Will it not be received,
	When we have marked with blood those sleepy two 75
	Of his own chamber, and used their very daggers,
	That they have done't?
LADY MACBETH	Who dares receive it other? –
	As we shall make our griefs and clamour roar
	Upon his death?
MACBETH	I am settled – and bend up
	Each corporal agent to this terrible feat. 80
	Away, and mock the time with fairest show! –
	False face must hide what the false heart doth know.

Exeunt.

Act 2   Scene 1

In this scene ...

- Macbeth tries to test Banquo to see how loyal he might be to him in the future.
- Once Banquo has left, Macbeth has a vision of a dagger stained with blood.
- Macbeth goes to kill Duncan.

Banquo, who is being kept awake by troubling thoughts, is walking outside with his son, Fleance. He meets Macbeth, and tells him how grateful Duncan is for his and Lady Macbeth's hospitality. Banquo mentions their meeting with the Witches.

THINK ABOUT for GCSE

Characterisation

- What 'cursèd thoughts' (line 8) are preventing Banquo from sleeping? Look at lines 20 to 21, for example.

Language

- Look at the image in lines 4 to 5. What idea does it convey? What atmosphere does it help to create at the opening of this scene?

2 **is down**: has set

4 **husbandry**: good house-keeping
5 **candles**: i.e. stars
6–7 **A heavy ... sleep**: I am desperate to sleep, but I don't want to
8–9 **that ... repose**: which enter my head when I rest

13 **been ... pleasure**: had a particularly enjoyable time
14 **largess**: gifts
    offices: servants' quarters
16 **shut up**: went to bed
17 **in measureless content**: extremely happy
17–19 **Being ... wrought**: As we were not prepared for his visit, we could not give as warm a welcome as we would have liked

52

Inverness: the castle courtyard.

Enter BANQUO, *and his son* FLEANCE. *A servant carries a burning torch to light their way.*

BANQUO	How goes the night, boy?
FLEANCE	The moon is down. I have not heard the clock.
BANQUO	And she goes down at twelve.
FLEANCE	I take 't, 'tis later, sir.
BANQUO	Hold, take my sword. – There's husbandry in heaven:

Banquo (continued):
Their candles are all out. – Take thee that, too.   5
A heavy summons lies like lead upon me,
And yet I would not sleep. Merciful powers! –
Restrain in me the cursèd thoughts that nature
Gives way to in repose! – Give me my sword.

Enter MACBETH, *also with a torch-bearer.*

Who's there?   10

MACBETH A friend.

BANQUO What, sir! Not yet at rest? The King's a-bed.
He hath been in unusual pleasure, and
Sent forth great largess to your offices.
This diamond he greets your wife withal,   15
By the name of most kind hostess – and shut up
In measureless content.

MACBETH Being unprepared,
Our will became the servant to defect,
Which else should free have wrought.

BANQUO All's well.
I dreamt last night of the three weird sisters.   20
To you they have showed some truth.

Banquo cautiously says that he is loyal to the King and leaves to go to bed. Left alone, Macbeth suddenly has a vision of a blood-stained dagger.

22 **entreat ... serve**: find a convenient time

24 **At ... leisure**: Whenever it is convenient for you

25 **If ... 'tis**: If you will stay on my side (or follow my advice) when the time comes

26–7 **So ... augment it**: As long as I don't lose honour by trying to gain more

27–8 **still ... clear**: always keep my conscience clear and my loyalty to the King unstained

29 **shall be counselled**: i.e. am willing to listen
Good ... while: Meanwhile, sleep well

THINK ABOUT for GCSE

Performance and staging

- If you were the director, would you make this conversation between Macbeth and Banquo friendly and warm, or cold and formal? Why?

- How would you represent Macbeth's vision of the dagger in (a) a theatre production; and (b) a film? Think about its position as he sees it, its changing appearance, and the way it behaves. What effect does it have on the audience if we do not see it at all?

36 **have thee not**: can't grasp you

37–8 **sensible ... sight**: able to be touched as well as seen

40 **heat-oppressèd**: feverish

41 **palpable**: apparently touchable

42 **this**: i.e. Macbeth's own dagger

43 **Thou marshall'st**: You direct

45 **Mine ... senses**: Either my eyes are foolish compared with all the other senses

47 **dudgeon**: handle
gouts: drops

49–50 **informs ... eyes**: is making me see things like this

MACBETH	I think not of them.

Yet, when we can entreat an hour to serve,
We would spend it in some words upon that business,
If you would grant the time.

BANQUO	At your kind'st leisure.

MACBETH   If you shall cleave to my consent, when 'tis,   25
It shall make honour for you.

BANQUO	So I lose none

In seeking to augment it, but still keep
My bosom franchised, and allegiance clear,
I shall be counselled.

MACBETH	Good repose the while!

BANQUO   Thanks, sir: the like to you.   30

Exit BANQUO, *with* FLEANCE *and their torch-bearer.*

MACBETH   (*To the servant carrying his torch*)
Go, bid thy mistress, when my drink is ready,
She strike upon the bell. Get thee to bed.

Exit servant.

Is this a dagger which I see before me,
The handle toward my hand?
Come, let me clutch thee. –   35
I have thee not – and yet I see thee still!
Art thou not, fatal vision, sensible
To feeling as to sight? Or art thou but
A dagger of the mind, a false creation,
Proceeding from the heat-oppressèd brain?   40
I see thee yet! – in form as palpable
As this which now I draw.
Thou marshall'st me the way that I was going –
And such an instrument I was to use.
Mine eyes are made the fools o' the other senses,   45
Or else worth all the rest. I see thee still! –
And on thy blade and dudgeon gouts of blood,
Which was not so before. – There's no such thing!
It is the bloody business which informs
Thus to mine eyes. – Now o'er the one half world   50

Afraid of making any noise that might be heard by the sleeping household, Macbeth goes to murder Duncan.

51 **abuse**: deceive / disturb

53 **Hecate**: the goddess of witchcraft
54 **Alarumed**: called into action
sentinel: sentry / watchman
55 **whose ... watch**: i.e. the wolf's howl is like the watchman's hourly call
56–7 **With ... ghost**: Murder is imagined as the legendary rapist Tarquin, moving silently towards his act of violence.
59 **prate ... whereabout**: gossip about where I am going
60–1 **take ... it**: i.e. break the horrifying silence of the night, which suits what I am going to do
61 **Whiles ... lives**: While I stand here talking about murder, Duncan remains alive
62 **Words ... gives**: words cool down the passion of actions
64 **knell**: funeral bell

THINK ABOUT for GCSE

Language

- What image does Macbeth have of 'Murder' (lines 53 to 57)? What meanings does it convey to you?

Characterisation

- What does his vision of a dagger suggest about Macbeth's state of mind?
- What does this image, and his prayer to 'earth' (lines 57 to 61), tell us about his attitude to what he has to do?

Nature seems dead, and wicked dreams abuse
The curtained sleep. Witchcraft celebrates
Pale Hecate's offerings. And withered Murder,
Alarumed by his sentinel, the wolf,
Whose howl's his watch, thus with his stealthy pace,   **55**
With Tarquin's ravishing strides, towards his design
Moves like a ghost. – Thou sure and firm-set earth,
Hear not my steps, which way they walk, for fear
Thy very stones prate of my whereabout,
And take the present horror from the time,   **60**
Which now suits with it. Whiles I threat, he lives:
Words to the heat of deeds too cold breath gives.

A bell rings.

I go, and it is done. The bell invites me.
Hear it not, Duncan – for it is a knell
That summons thee to heaven or to hell.

Exit.

In this scene ...

- Macbeth returns from Duncan's chamber and tells Lady Macbeth how he killed the King.
- Lady Macbeth is appalled to see that Macbeth has brought the bloody daggers away from Duncan's chamber. As he is too frightened to take them back, she does it herself.
- Hearing a knocking at the castle gates, Macbeth and Lady Macbeth go to wash the blood from their hands.

Lady Macbeth has drugged the attendants and has left their daggers ready for Macbeth to use to kill the sleeping King Duncan. Macbeth comes back to report that he has murdered him.

THINK ABOUT for GCSE

Language

- Sometimes a single line of verse is split between speakers. What is the dramatic effect of breaking up line 16 into four short speeches, three of which are questions? In what ways does it add to the tension? What does it show about the state of mind of the two characters? Think about how the actors might deliver those speeches.

2 **quenched them**: i.e. made them unconscious

3 **fatal bellman**: man who rang the bell before an execution or during a funeral

4 **stern'st**: harshest (because the owl's hoot signals that someone is about to die)

about it: performing the murder

5–6 **the surfeited ... charge**: Duncan's attendants, who have drunk too much, make a mockery of their job

6 **possets**: late-night alcoholic drinks

7–8 **That ... die**: i.e. so that they seem half dead

11 **Confounds us**: causes our downfall

13 **had done 't**: would have done it

15 **crickets**: Their chirping was thought to foretell death.

Inside the castle.

Enter LADY MACBETH, *alone.*

LADY MACBETH	That which hath made them drunk hath made me bold.
	What hath quenched them hath given me fire. – Hark!
	– Peace!
	It was the owl that shrieked, the fatal bellman,
	Which gives the stern'st goodnight. He is about it!
	The doors are open, and the surfeited grooms
	Do mock their charge with snores. I have drugged
	their possets –
	That death and nature do contend about them,
	Whether they live or die.

5

MACBETH	(*Calling from a distance*) Who's there? – What, ho!
LADY MACBETH	Alack! I am afraid they have awaked,
	And 'tis not done. The attempt and not the deed
	Confounds us! – Hark! – I laid their daggers ready:
	He could not miss them! – Had he not resembled
	My father as he slept, *I* had done 't. – My husband!

10

Enter MACBETH (*with two bloodstained daggers*).

MACBETH	I have done the deed. – Didst thou not hear a noise?
LADY MACBETH	I heard the owl scream, and the crickets cry.
	Did not you speak?

15

MACBETH	When?
LADY MACBETH	Now.
MACBETH	As I descended?
LADY MACBETH	Ay.
MACBETH	Hark! Who lies i' the second chamber?
LADY MACBETH	Donalbain.
MACBETH	(*Looking at his bloody hands*) This is a sorry sight.
LADY MACBETH	A foolish thought, to say a sorry sight.

Macbeth is greatly shaken
because he could not say
'Amen' and because he heard
a voice tell him that he would
never be able to sleep again.
Lady Macbeth is shocked that
he has brought the blood-
stained daggers away with him.

THINK ABOUT for**GCSE**

Performance and staging

* If you were directing a film
  of *Macbeth*, would you
  show the scene in which
  Macbeth murders Duncan
  (as Macbeth describes it in
  lines 19 to 40)? Think about
  what you would gain by
  showing it, and what you
  would lose.

Characterisation

* In what ways have Macbeth
  and Lady Macbeth already
  been affected by the murder
  of the King?

21 **That**: so that
22 **addressed them**: got ready

23 **lodged together**: sleeping in the same
    room

25 **As**: as if
    hangman's hands: executioner's
    bloody hands

28 **wherefore**: why

31 **After**: in

32 **Methought**: It seemed to me

34 **ravelled sleave**: tangled thread
35 **sore … bath**: i.e. sleep eases the aches
    caused by hard work
36 **Balm of**: soothing oil for
    second course: the main course in a
    meal

39 **Glamis … Cawdor**: Macbeth is Thane
    of Glamis and Thane of Cawdor.

41 **unbend**: weaken
43 **brainsickly**: feverishly
44 **filthy witness**: evidence of horrible
    deeds

MACBETH	There's one did laugh in's sleep, and one cried
	'Murder!', 20
	That they did wake each other. I stood and heard them.
	But they did say their prayers, and addressed them
	Again to sleep.

LADY MACBETH	There are two lodged together.

MACBETH	One cried, 'God bless us!' and 'Amen', the other –
	As they had seen me with these hangman's hands. 25
	Listening their fear, I could not say 'Amen',
	When they did say 'God bless us!'

LADY MACBETH	Consider it not so deeply.

MACBETH	But wherefore could not I pronounce 'Amen'?
	I had most need of blessing, and 'Amen'
	Stuck in my throat.

LADY MACBETH	These deeds must not be thought 30
	After these ways: so, it will make us mad.

MACBETH	Methought I heard a voice cry, 'Sleep no more! –
	Macbeth does murder sleep!' – the innocent sleep –
	Sleep that knits up the ravelled sleave of care,
	The death of each day's life, sore labour's bath, 35
	Balm of hurt minds, great nature's second course,
	Chief nourisher in life's feast –

LADY MACBETH	What do you mean?

MACBETH	Still it cried, 'Sleep no more!' to all the house:
	'Glamis hath murdered sleep – and therefore Cawdor
	Shall sleep no more. Macbeth shall sleep no more!' 40

LADY MACBETH	Who was it that thus cried? Why, worthy thane,
	You do unbend your noble strength, to think
	So brainsickly of things. Go, get some water,
	And wash this filthy witness from your hand. –
	Why did you bring these daggers from the place? 45
	They must lie there! Go, carry them, and smear
	The sleepy grooms with blood.

MACBETH	I'll go no more.
	I am afraid to think what I have done.
	Look on't again I dare not.

Lady Macbeth angrily takes the daggers back herself because Macbeth refuses to. They hear a knocking at the castle gates. They go to wash the blood from their hands, Macbeth already regretting what he has done.

THINK ABOUT for GCSE

Characterisation

• What does Macbeth's reaction in lines 14 to 40 to the sounds he has heard (or thinks he has heard) suggest about his state of mind? Look at line 55, for example.

Structure and form

• Lady Macbeth says, 'A little water clears us of this deed' (line 64). In what ways might this be viewed as dramatic irony?

Language

• What do you think Macbeth means by 'To know my deed, 'twere best not know myself' (line 70)?

49   **Infirm of purpose**: Weak-willed man

51–2   **'tis … devil**: i.e. only children are frightened of pictures

53   **gild**: paint (with gold)

54   **seem their guilt**: i.e. look as though they have committed the murder

54   **Whence … knocking**: Where's that knocking coming from

56   **They … eyes**: i.e. he wants to pull his eyes out so that they can no longer see his bloody hands

57   **Neptune**: the Roman god of the sea

58–60   **this … red**: my hand is more likely to turn the countless green seas blood red

62   **white**: i.e. cowardly

63   **Retire … chamber**: Let's go to our bedroom

65   **constancy … unattended**: firmness of purpose has deserted you

67–8   **lest … watchers**: in case people call us and realise we have been up and awake

71   **I … couldst**: I wish you could

LADY MACBETH	Infirm of purpose!

LADY MACBETH   Infirm of purpose!
Give me the daggers! The sleeping and the dead   50
Are but as pictures: 'tis the eye of childhood
That fears a painted devil. If he do bleed,
I'll gild the faces of the grooms withal,
For it must seem their guilt.

Exit.

A knocking is heard.

MACBETH   Whence is that knocking? –
How is't with me, when every noise appals me?   55
What hands are here? Ha! They pluck out mine eyes!
Will all great Neptune's ocean wash this blood
Clean from my hand? No – this my hand will rather
The multitudinous seas incarnadine,
Making the green one red.   60

Re-enter LADY MACBETH.

LADY MACBETH My hands are of your colour – but I shame
To wear a heart so white! (*Knocking heard again*)
   I hear a knocking
At the south entry. Retire we to our chamber.
A little water clears us of this deed:
How easy is it then! Your constancy   65
Hath left you unattended. (*Knocking again*) Hark! –
   more knocking.
Get on your night-gown, lest occasion call us,
And show us to be watchers. – Be not lost
So poorly in your thoughts!

MACBETH To know my deed, 'twere best not know myself.   70

Knocking heard again.

Wake Duncan with thy knocking! I would thou couldst!

Exeunt.

In this scene ...

- The castle porter opens the gates to Macduff and Lennox and jokes with them.
- Having gone to wake the King, Macduff discovers the murder. Duncan's sons, Malcolm and Donalbain, are told of their father's death.
- As Macbeth is explaining that he killed the attendants because he was furious that they had killed Duncan, his wife faints.
- Malcolm and Donalbain, fearing for their safety, decide to flee.

The castle porter imagines himself to be the porter of the gates of hell, welcoming in various types of sinner. He opens the gates to let in Macduff and Lennox.

THINK ABOUT for GCSE

Structure and form

- What effect does the entrance of the Porter, a comic character, have at this point in the play?

Context

- In May 1606, the year *Macbeth* was probably written, a priest, Father Henry Garnett was executed for his part in the 'Gunpowder Plot'. Garnett claimed that it was acceptable to equivocate if it was for a good object. What view of equivocators does the Porter's speech suggest?

2 **old**: plenty of

4 **Beelzebub**: the devil

5 **plenty**: a good harvest
 time-server: somebody who 1 depends on the seasons; 2 will serve time in hell

6 **napkins**: handkerchiefs (to mop up the sweat in hell)

7–8 **other devil**: probably Satan

8 **equivocator**: someone who deceives by telling half-truths

9 **swear ... scale**: balance up the scales of Justice by arguing on both sides

10 **treason**: betraying your King or country

14 **stealing ... hose**: i.e. using less cloth than the customers had paid for

14–15 **roast your goose**: 1 heat your flat-iron; 2 sweat out your diseased body

18–19 **primrose ... bonfire**: i.e. attractive path to hell

20 **Anon**: I'm coming
 remember: i.e. give a tip to

21 **ere**: before

23 **carousing ... cock**: drinking until three in the morning

24 **provoker**: encourager

26 **Marry**: Indeed (By Saint Mary)
 nose-painting: getting a red nose (through drink)
 Lechery: Wanting to have sex

28 **takes ... performance**: i.e. makes you incapable of having sex

The castle courtyard.

Knocking heard again.

Enter the PORTER *of the gate.*

PORTER Here's a knocking indeed! If a man were porter of hell-gate, he should have old turning the key. (*Knocking again*) Knock, knock, knock. Who's there, i' the name of Beelzebub? – Here's a farmer that hanged himself on the expectation of plenty. Come in, time-server. Have   5
napkins enough about you: here you'll sweat for it. (*Knocking again*) Knock, knock! Who's there, i' the other devil's name? – 'Faith, here's an equivocator that could swear in both the scales against either scale – who committed treason enough for God's sake, yet could not   10
equivocate to heaven. O, come in, equivocator! (*Knocking again*) Knock, knock, knock. Who's there? – 'Faith, here's an English tailor, come hither for stealing out of a French hose. Come in, tailor! Here you may roast your goose. (*Knocking again*) Knock, knock.   15
Never at quiet! What are you? – But this place is too cold for hell. I'll devil-porter it no further. I had thought to have let in some of all professions that go the primrose way to the everlasting bonfire. (*Knocking again*) Anon, anon! I pray you, remember the porter.   20

He opens the gate.

Enter MACDUFF *and* LENNOX.

MACDUFF Was it so late, friend, ere you went to bed,
That you do lie so late?

PORTER 'Faith, sir, we were carousing till the second cock – and drink, sir, is a great provoker of three things.

MACDUFF What three things does drink especially provoke?   25

PORTER Marry, sir, nose-painting, sleep and urine. Lechery, sir, it provokes and unprovokes: it provokes the desire, but it takes away the performance. Therefore, much drink may

The Porter jokes with Macduff and Lennox about the effects of alcohol. Macbeth enters and tells Macduff where the King's room is, because Duncan had asked Macduff to wake him.

29   **equivocator with**: deceiver of
30   **mars**: ruins
30–2   **it sets … stand to**: i.e. it gives him a sexual appetite but makes him incapable of satisfying it
33   **giving him the lie**: 1 deceiving him; 2 making him lie down; 3 making him urinate
35   **i' the … o' me**: 1 by lying to my face; 2 by being poured down my throat
       requited him: paid him back
37   **took up my legs**: i.e. made me fall over
       made a shift: managed
38   **cast**: 1 throw (as in wrestling); 2 throw up

THINK ABOUT *for* GCSE

Performance and staging

• If you were performing the Porter, which parts would you make comic and which serious?

Themes and issues

• The Porter imagines welcoming an 'equivocator' to hell (lines 8 to 11) and says that drink is 'an equivocator with lechery' (lines 29 to 33). What examples of **equivocation** – the use of ambiguity (double meanings) to conceal the truth – have you encountered in the play so far?

43   **timely**: early
44   **slipped**: missed

45–6   **joyful … one**: i.e. because Macbeth has been pleased to have the King in his castle, even though the visit has caused extra work
47   **The … pain**: Work that we enjoy is a cure for any hardship it causes
49   **my limited service**: what I was asked to do

50   **Goes … hence**: Is the King leaving

be said to be an equivocator with lechery: it makes him
and it mars him; it sets him on, and it takes him off; it   **30**
persuades him, and disheartens him; makes him stand
to, and not stand to. In conclusion, equivocates him in
a sleep, and, giving him the lie, leaves him.

MACDUFF   I believe drink gave thee the lie last night.

PORTER   That it did, sir, i' the very throat o' me. But I requited   **35**
               him for his lie – and, I think, being too strong for him,
               though he took up my legs sometime, yet I made a shift
               to cast him.

MACDUFF   Is thy master stirring?

Enter MACBETH.

               Our knocking has awaked him: here he comes.   **40**

LENNOX   Good morrow, noble sir!

MACBETH   Good morrow, both!

                                            Exit the PORTER.

MACDUFF   Is the King stirring, worthy Thane?

MACBETH   Not yet.

MACDUFF   He did command me to call timely on him:
               I have almost slipped the hour.

MACBETH   I'll bring you to him.

MACDUFF   I know this is a joyful trouble to you;   **45**
               But yet 'tis one.

MACBETH   The labour we delight in physics pain.
               This is the door.

MACDUFF   I'll make so bold to call,
               For 'tis my limited service.

                                                    Exit.

LENNOX   Goes the King hence today?

MACBETH   He does. – He did appoint so.   **50**

As Lennox is describing the strange, unnatural events of the previous night, Macduff comes back crying out in horror because he has discovered Duncan's murder.

51 **unruly**: wild and stormy

53 **Lamentings**: cries of misery
54 **prophesying ... terrible**: forecasting in a horrifying way
55 **dire ... events**: terrible confusion and chaos
56 **New hatched to**: born out of
    obscure bird: owl
57 **Clamoured**: i.e. hooted
59–60 **My young ... it**: I cannot recall a night like it in my young life

62 **conceive**: imagine

63 **Confusion**: Destruction
64 **sacrilegious**: unholy
    ope: open
65 **Lord's anointed temple**: i.e. the King's body

THINK ABOUT *for* GCSE

Context

- What impact might Lennox's speech (lines 51 to 58) have had in Shakespeare's time? Think about lines 63 to 66 and the beliefs Shakespeare's audience would have had about omens and kingship. What significance might Lennox have attached to the night's events?

69 **Gorgon**: In Greek mythology, anyone who looked at the Gorgon was turned to stone.

73 **downy**: comfortable
    death's counterfeit: i.e. sleep
75 **The ... image**: a sight as terrifying as the Last Judgement (when the souls of the dead will finally be judged)
76 **sprites**: spirits
77 **countenance**: 1 face; 2 be in keeping with

LENNOX	The night has been unruly. Where we lay,
	Our chimneys were blown down – and, as they say,
	Lamentings heard i' the air – strange screams of death,
	And prophesying with accents terrible
	Of dire combustion, and confused events, 55
	New hatched to the woeful time. The obscure bird
	Clamoured the livelong night. Some say the earth
	Was feverous, and did shake.

MACBETH   'Twas a rough night.

LENNOX	My young remembrance cannot parallel
	A fellow to it. 60

Re-enter MACDUFF.

MACDUFF	O horror! Horror! Horror! Tongue, nor heart,
	Cannot conceive, nor name thee!

MACBETH   What's the matter?
and LENNOX

MACDUFF	Confusion now hath made his masterpiece!
	Most sacrilegious murder hath broke ope
	The Lord's anointed temple, and stole thence 65
	The life o' the building!

MACBETH   What is't you say? – the life?

LENNOX   Mean you his majesty?

MACDUFF	Approach the chamber, and destroy your sight
	With a new Gorgon. – Do not bid me speak:
	See, and then speak yourselves. –

Exit MACBETH, *with* LENNOX.

Awake! Awake! –   70
Ring the alarum-bell! – Murder and treason!
Banquo and Donalbain! Malcolm! Awake!
Shake off this downy sleep, death's counterfeit,
And look on death itself! – Up, up, and see
The great doom's image! – Malcolm! Banquo!   75
As from your graves rise up, and walk like sprites
To countenance this horror!

Ringing of the alarm bell is heard.

Lady Macbeth and Banquo are told that Duncan has been murdered. Macbeth expresses shock. When Duncan's sons, Malcolm and Donalbain, enter they are told that their father has been killed.

78 to parley: for a conference

81–2 The repetition … fell: Reporting it to a woman would kill her

85 prithee: beg you

87 chance: happening

89 serious in mortality: important in human life (or death)
90 toys: trivial things
    renown and grace: fame and good deeds
91 drawn: taken from the barrel
    the mere lees: only the dregs
92 vault: wine cellar, i.e. the world
    brag of: boast about
93 What is amiss: What's wrong
94 The spring … blood: i.e. your father
95 stopped: i.e. dead

THINK ABOUT for GCSE

Performance and staging

- If you were the director, how would you ask the actors playing (a) Lady Macbeth; (b) Banquo; (c) Macbeth; and (d) Macduff, to react when they hear of the murder?

Language

- What idea is Macbeth conveying in lines 91 to 92? How effective is the image he uses in getting that idea across?

Enter LADY MACBETH.

LADY MACBETH   What's the business,
    That such a hideous trumpet calls to parley
    The sleepers of the house? Speak, speak!

MACDUFF   O gentle lady,
    'Tis not for you to hear what I can speak.   80
    The repetition, in a woman's ear,
    Would murder as it fell. –

Enter BANQUO.

                    O Banquo! Banquo!
    Our royal master's murdered!

LADY MACBETH   Woe, alas!
    What! In our house?

BANQUO   Too cruel anywhere!
    Dear Duff, I prithee contradict thyself   85
    And say it is not so.

Re-enter MACBETH *and* LENNOX.

MACBETH   Had I but died an hour before this chance,
    I had lived a blessèd time – for, from this instant,
    There's nothing serious in mortality.
    All is but toys: renown and grace is dead –   90
    The wine of life is drawn, and the mere lees
    Is left this vault to brag of.

Enter MALCOLM *and* DONALBAIN.

DONALBAIN   What is amiss?

MACBETH   You are, and do not know it.
    The spring, the head, the fountain of your blood
    Is stopped: the very source of it is stopped.   95

MACDUFF   Your royal father's murdered.

MALCOLM   O! By whom?

Lennox says that it seems that Duncan was killed by the attendants in his room. Macbeth claims that he killed the attendants in his fury. As he goes on to describe how he saw the murdered Duncan, Lady Macbeth faints. Malcolm and Donalbain privately share their fears for their own safety.

THINK ABOUT for GCSE

Performance and staging

- In a performance, Lady Macbeth's faint (line 114) can be acted as though either genuine or fake. If you were the director, how would you want to show it, and why?

Language

- Macbeth's language here is complex and full of images, but the language of the other characters is more straightforward. What could account for this contrast?

98   **badged**: marked, i.e. blood was the 'badge' which showed that they were murderers

100   **distracted**: behaved as if mad

103   **Wherefore**: Why

104   **temperate**: level-headed

106–7   **The expedition … reason**: My passionate love for the King made me act hastily, before reason could make me stop and think

108   **laced**: i.e. streaked

109   **breach**: gaping hole

111   **Steeped**: dyed
        colours … trade: i.e. blood-red

112   **Unmannerly … gore**: indecently clothed with blood
        refrain: restrain himself

114   **make's**: make his

116   **That … ours**: when we are the ones most closely affected by what's happened

118   **auger-hole**: tiny drill-hole

119–20   **Our … brewed**: i.e. We are not ready to weep yet

121   **Upon … motion**: i.e. ready to show itself

122   **our … hid**: i.e. got dressed

125   **scruples**: doubts

LENNOX	Those of his chamber, as it seemed, had done it.

LENNOX   Those of his chamber, as it seemed, had done it.
          Their hands and faces were all badged with blood:
          So were their daggers, which, unwiped, we found
          Upon their pillows. They stared, and were distracted.   100
          No man's life was to be trusted with them.

MACBETH   O, yet I do repent me of my fury –
          That I did kill them.

MACDUFF   Wherefore did you so?

MACBETH   Who can be wise, amazed, temperate and furious,
          Loyal and neutral, in a moment? No man!   105
          The expedition of my violent love
          Outran the pauser reason. – Here lay Duncan,
          His silver skin laced with his golden blood!
          And his gashed stabs looked like a breach in nature
          For ruin's wasteful entrance. There, the murderers,   110
          Steeped in the colours of their trade! – their daggers
          Unmannerly breeched with gore. Who could refrain,
          That had a heart to love – and in that heart
          Courage, to make's love known?

LADY MACBETH   (*Fainting*) Help me hence, ho!

MACDUFF   Look to the lady!

MALCOLM   (*Aside to* DONALBAIN) Why do we hold our tongues,   115
          That most may claim this argument for ours?

DONALBAIN (*Aside to* MALCOLM) What should be spoken
          Here – where our fate, hid in an auger-hole,
          May rush and seize us? Let's away. Our tears
          Are not yet brewed.

MALCOLM   (*Aside to* DONALBAIN) Nor our strong sorrow   120
          Upon the foot of motion.

BANQUO   Look to the lady! –

LADY MACBETH *is helped away.*

          And when we have our naked frailties hid
          That suffer in exposure, let us meet,
          And question this most bloody piece of work,
          To know it further. Fears and scruples shake us.   125

When everyone else has gone to get dressed, Malcolm and Donalbain discuss what to do. Malcolm decides to flee to England, Donalbain to Ireland. Malcolm fears that there will be more killings.

126–8 In … malice: I put myself under God's protection and, relying on God, I will fight against the hidden purposes of wicked traitors

129 briefly: quickly
put … readiness: 1 get properly dressed; 2 adopt a warlike frame of mind

131 consort: keep company
132 office: action
133 false: deceitful

134–5 Our … safer: We will be safer if we are not together
136–7 the near … bloody: the more closely we are related to these deceitful people, the more chance we have of being murdered
137–8 shaft … lighted: arrow has not yet hit its target
140 dainty of leave-taking: fussy about saying goodbye properly
141 shift away: slip away
141–2 There's … left: When there are merciless people around, slipping away is justifiable

THINK ABOUT for GCSE

Characterisation

- What does Banquo's response to the situation reveal about him (lines 121 to 128)?

Structure and form

- Do you think Malcolm and Donalbain have a good idea about who murdered their father? Why?

- What do you think about Malcolm and Donalbain's decision to flee, and for Malcolm to go to England, Donalbain to Ireland?
Try to predict what further part, if any, they might play in the plot.

In the great hand of God I stand – and thence
Against the undivulged pretence I fight
Of treasonous malice.

MACDUFF   And so do I.

ALL   So all.

MACBETH   Let's briefly put on manly readiness,
And meet i' the hall together.

ALL   Well contented.   130

Exit MACBETH, *with* MACDUFF, BANQUO *and* LENNOX.
MALCOLM *and* DONALBAIN *remain.*

MALCOLM   What will you do? Let's not consort with them.
To show an unfelt sorrow is an office
Which the false man does easy. I'll to England.

DONALBAIN To Ireland, I. Our separated fortune
Shall keep us both the safer. Where we are   135
There's daggers in men's smiles: the near in blood,
The nearer bloody.

MALCOLM   This murderous shaft that's shot
Hath not yet lighted, and our safest way
Is to avoid the aim. Therefore to horse,
And let us not be dainty of leave-taking,   140
But shift away. There's warrant in that theft
Which steals itself, when there's no mercy left.

Exeunt.

In this scene ...

- An old man and Ross discuss the strange, unnatural events which have followed the killing of Duncan.
- Macduff joins them. He reports that Duncan's sons, Malcolm and Donalbain, are said to have bribed their father's attendants to kill him.
- While Macduff decides to return to his castle in Fife, Ross goes to see Macbeth crowned as King.

Ross and an old man talk about the disturbing unnatural events that have followed King Duncan's murder.

THINK ABOUT for GCSE

Themes and issues

- Which events described here seem to be an inversion of the **natural order**?
- **Order and nature:** Which other happenings in the play are 'against nature'? Look back at Act 1 Scene 3, lines 137 to 138, and Act 1 Scene 5, lines 39 to 53, for example.

Context

- In Shakespeare's theatre, the 'heavens' – stars, moon and sun – were possibly painted on the underside of the canopy over the stage. What is Ross suggesting by his playhouse imagery in lines 5 and 6?

1 **Threescore and ten**: Seventy years
2 **volume**: space
3 **sore**: dreadful
4 **trifled ... knowings**: made everything I have experienced before seem trivial
  father: a term of respect to an old man
5–6 **Thou ... stage**: i.e. the heavens, as though disturbed by men's actions, are now threatening the earth
7 **travelling lamp**: i.e. the sun
8 **Is't ... shame**: Is it the superior power of night, or is the day hiding its face in shame
9 **entomb**: cover, as though in a dark tomb
12 **towering ... place**: rising to her highest point
13 **by ... killed**: i.e. the owl, which normally preyed only on small creatures, attacked a (fiercer) falcon
15 **minions of their race**: the best of their breed
17 **Contending ... obedience**: rebelling against their training
  as: as if

Act 2 Scene 4

Inverness: outside the castle.

Enter Ross, *with an* Old Man.

OLD MAN   Threescore and ten I can remember well –
            Within the volume of which time I have seen
            Hours dreadful and things strange. But this sore night
            Hath trifled former knowings.

ROSS   Ha, good father,
            Thou see'st the heavens, as troubled with man's act,   5
            Threatens his bloody stage. By the clock 'tis day,
            And yet dark night strangles the travelling lamp.
            Is't night's predominance, or the day's shame,
            That darkness does the face of earth entomb,
            When living light should kiss it?

OLD MAN   'Tis unnatural –   10
            Even like the deed that's done. On Tuesday last,
            A falcon, towering in her pride of place,
            Was by a mousing owl hawked at, and killed.

ROSS   And Duncan's horses (a thing most strange and certain),
            Beauteous and swift, the minions of their race,   15
            Turned wild in nature, broke their stalls, flung out,
            Contending 'gainst obedience, as they would make
            War with mankind.

OLD MAN   'Tis said, they ate each other.

ROSS   They did so, to th' amazement of mine eyes,
            That looked upon it. –

Enter Macduff.

                                 Here comes the good Macduff. –   20
            How goes the world, sir, now?

MACDUFF   Why, see you not?

ROSS   Is't known who did this more than bloody deed?

MACDUFF   Those that Macbeth hath slain.

Macduff says that the attendants are reported to have killed Duncan on Malcolm's and Donalbain's orders. He says that Macbeth has already gone to Scone to be crowned, but that he himself is not going to attend the coronation.

24   **What ... pretend**: What could they hope to gain by it
       suborned: bribed to commit the crime

27   **'Gainst nature still**: Yet another example of unnatural events
28–9 **Thriftless ... means**: Pointless ambition, which will gobble up the body that gives you life
29   **like**: likely that
30   **sovereignty**: title of King
31   **named**: chosen as King
       Scone: The place where Scottish kings were crowned.
32   **invested**: crowned
33   **Colme-kill**: The island of Iona, where Scottish kings were buried.

36   **thither**: go there (to the coronation)
37   **Adieu**: Goodbye

40   **benison**: blessing

THINK ABOUT for GCSE

Characterisation

- What do you think Macduff feels about the theory that Duncan's sons bribed his attendants to kill their father?
- What evidence is there that Macduff is unhappy at the idea of Macbeth becoming King?

Language

- What does Macduff mean in lines 37 to 38? How effective is the clothing imagery he uses in getting the point across?

ROSS	Alas, the day! What good could they pretend?
MACDUFF	They were suborned. Malcolm and Donalbain, the King's two sons, **25** Are stol'n away and fled – which puts upon them Suspicion of the deed.
ROSS	'Gainst nature still! Thriftless ambition, that wilt ravin up Thine own life's means! – Then 'tis most like The sovereignty will fall upon Macbeth. **30**
MACDUFF	He is already named, and gone to Scone To be invested.
ROSS	Where is Duncan's body?
MACDUFF	Carried to Colme-kill – The sacred storehouse of his predecessors, And guardian of their bones.
ROSS	Will you to Scone? **35**
MACDUFF	No, cousin: I'll to Fife.
ROSS	Well, I will thither.
MACDUFF	Well, may you see things well done there. – Adieu! – Lest our old robes sit easier than our new!
ROSS	Farewell, father.
OLD MAN	God's benison go with you – and with those **40** That would make good of bad, and friends of foes!

Exeunt.

In this scene ...

- Banquo privately says that he is suspicious of Macbeth.
- Macbeth and Lady Macbeth – now the King and Queen – greet Banquo. Macbeth checks on Banquo's plans to go riding that afternoon.
- Macbeth privately expresses his fears about Banquo. He knows that Banquo is a good man, and he cannot forget the Witches' prophecy that Banquo's descendants will be kings.
- He persuades two murderers to kill Banquo and his son, Fleance.

Banquo expresses his fear that Macbeth must have murdered Duncan. He wonders whether the Witches' prophecy for himself will come true. To gain information about Banquo's movements, Macbeth asks him whether he plans to go riding that afternoon.

1   **it**: i.e. the crown
3   **Thou ... foully**: you played a very dirty game
4   **It ... posterity**: the crown would not be passed on to your descendants
6   **them**: i.e. the Witches
7   **shine**: are brilliantly fulfilled
8   **verities ... good**: things that have come true for you
9   **oracles**: i.e. like the ancient priestesses who foretold what would happen

13 **all-thing unbecoming**: completely inappropriate
14 **solemn**: ceremonial

THINK ABOUT for GCSE

Performance and staging

- If you were the director, how would you ask the actor playing Banquo to deliver lines 1 to 10? Think about whether you would show him as a good man, deeply troubled by fears that Macbeth has murdered the King, or as an ambitious man who hopes that the prophecy made to him will now come true.

17–18 **with ... knit**: tied with a knot which cannot be broken

20 **else**: otherwise
21 **still**: always
    grave and prosperous: serious and profitable
22 **council**: meeting of the King and his advisors

Forres: inside the palace.

Enter BANQUO, *alone.*

BANQUO   Thou hast it now – King, Cawdor, Glamis, all,
As the weird women promised; and, I fear,
Thou playedst most foully for't. Yet it was said,
It should not stand in thy posterity;
But that myself should be the root and father   5
Of many kings. If there come truth from them
(As upon thee, Macbeth, their speeches shine),
Why, by the verities on thee made good,
May they not be my oracles as well,
And set me up in hope? But, hush: no more.   10

Trumpet fanfare. Enter MACBETH, *as King,* LADY MACBETH, *as Queen, with* LENNOX, ROSS, *other Lords, and attendants.*

MACBETH   Here's our chief guest.

LADY MACBETH   If he had been forgotten,
It had been as a gap in our great feast,
And all-thing unbecoming.

MACBETH   (*To* BANQUO) Tonight we hold a solemn supper, sir,
And I'll request your presence.

BANQUO   Let your Highness   15
Command upon me, to the which my duties
Are with a most indissoluble tie
For ever knit.

MACBETH   Ride you this afternoon?

BANQUO   Ay, my good lord.

MACBETH   We should have else desired your good advice   20
(Which still hath been both grave and prosperous)
In this day's council. But we'll take tomorrow.
Is't far you ride?

Macbeth asks Banquo whether his son, Fleance, will be going riding with him. Macbeth sends Lady Macbeth and the others away and gives voice to his fears about Banquo.

25 **go ... better**: if my horse doesn't go faster

26–7 **become ... twain**: have to take up an hour or two of the night

27 **Fail not**: Don't miss

29 **bloody cousins**: i.e. Malcolm and Donalbain (who, according to Macbeth, murdered their father)
bestowed: settled

31 **parricide**: killing of their father

32 **strange invention**: absurd lies

33 **therewithal**: in addition
cause: business

34 **Craving us jointly**: which we need to deal with together
Hie you: Hurry

36 **our ... upon 's**: it is time for us to go

40 **be ... time**: pass the time as he wishes

41 **society**: being with each other

43 **while**: until

44 **Sirrah**: i.e. You, there!

44–5 **Attend ... pleasure**: Are those men waiting to see me

46 **without**: outside

47 **thus**: i.e. King

49 **royalty of nature**: natural nobility

51 **to ... temper**: as well as that fearless spirit

52 **valour**: courage

THINK ABOUT for GCSE

Themes and issues

• **Deceit and equivocation**: Remember Lady Macbeth's advice to Macbeth to 'look like the innocent flower But be the serpent under 't' (Act 1 Scene 5, lines 64 to 65). Which three 'innocent' questions does Macbeth throw into his conversation with Banquo here?

BANQUO	As far, my lord, as will fill up the time
	'Twixt this and supper. Go not my horse the better, 25
	I must become a borrower of the night
	For a dark hour or twain.
MACBETH	Fail not our feast.
BANQUO	My lord, I will not.
MACBETH	We hear our bloody cousins are bestowed
	In England and in Ireland – not confessing 30
	Their cruel parricide, filling their hearers
	With strange invention. But of that tomorrow,
	When, therewithal, we shall have cause of state
	Craving us jointly. Hie you to horse. Adieu,
	Till you return at night. Goes Fleance with you? 35
BANQUO	Ay, my good lord: our time does call upon 's.
MACBETH	I wish your horses swift, and sure of foot;
	And so I do commend you to their backs.
	Farewell.

Exit BANQUO.

(*To the other lords*) Let every man be master of his time   40
Till seven at night. To make society
The sweeter welcome, we will keep ourself
Till supper-time alone: while then, God be with you.

Exit LADY MACBETH, **with** LENNOX, ROSS, *Lords, and attendants.*

(*To a servant*) Sirrah, a word with you. Attend those
    men
Our pleasure?   45

SERVANT	They are, my lord, without the palace gate.
MACBETH	Bring them before us. (*Exit* SERVANT, *leaving Macbeth alone.*) – To be thus is nothing,
	But to be safely thus! – Our fears in Banquo
	Stick deep – and in his royalty of nature
	Reigns that which would be feared. 'Tis much he dares – 50
	And, to that dauntless temper of his mind,
	He hath a wisdom that doth guide his valour
	To act in safety. There is none but he

Macbeth is tormented by the Witches' prophecy that Banquo's descendants will be kings of Scotland, and he has decided to take action. He calls in two murderers and convinces them that Banquo has always been their enemy.

54–5 **under … rebuked**: my guardian spirit is subdued by Banquo's

56 **chid**: spoke harshly to

58 **bade**: asked

60–1 **fruitless … sceptre**: i.e. no sons of Macbeth will become kings

61 **gripe**: grip

62 **Thence … hand**: to be torn from it by someone who is not one of my descendants

64 **issue**: descendants
filed: polluted

66 **rancours**: bitter thoughts
vessel … peace: my otherwise peaceful mind

67 **mine eternal jewel**: my immortal soul

68 **common … man**: i.e. the devil

70 **Rather than so**: Instead of letting that happen
list: tournament

71 **champion … utterance**: i.e. Macbeth is determined to fight the fate which has said that Banquo's offspring will be kings

THINK ABOUT for GCSE

Characterisation

• Look at Macbeth's speech (lines 47 to 71). What exactly are his fears about Banquo? What does Macbeth fear might have resulted from his murder of Duncan? How does he decide to deal with these fears?

76 *he*: i.e. Banquo

76–7 **which … fortune**: i.e. who stopped you enjoying the life you deserved

78 **made … you**: showed you convincingly

79 **passed in probation**: went over the proof

80 **borne … instruments**: deceived, obstructed, and what methods he used

81 **wrought with them**: was involved

82–3 **To … Banquo**: i.e. which even a half-wit or madman could see was Banquo's doing

Whose being I do fear – and under him
My genius is rebuked, as, it is said,   55
Mark Antony's was by Caesar. He chid the sisters
When first they put the name of king upon me,
And bade them speak to him. Then, prophet-like,
They hailed him father to a line of kings.
Upon my head they placed a fruitless crown,   60
And put a barren sceptre in my gripe,
Thence to be wrenched with an unlineal hand,
No son of mine succeeding. If 't be so,
For *Banquo's* issue have I filed my mind –
For them the gracious Duncan have I murdered;   65
Put rancours in the vessel of my peace
Only for them – and mine eternal jewel
Given to the common enemy of man,
To make them kings, the seed of Banquo kings!
Rather than so, come, Fate, into the list,   70
And champion me to the utterance! – Who's there? –

Re-enter the SERVANT, *bringing two* MURDERERS.

(*To the* SERVANT) Now go to the door, and stay there
   till we call.

Exit SERVANT.

Was it not yesterday we spoke together?

MURDERER 1   It was, so please your Highness.

MACBETH   Well then, now
Have you considered of my speeches? Know   75
That it was *he*, in the times past, which held you
So under fortune, which you thought had been
Our innocent self. This I made good to you
In our last conference; passed in probation with you
How you were borne in hand; how crossed, the
   instruments;   80
Who wrought with them – and all things else, that
   might
To half a soul, and to a notion crazed,
Say, 'Thus did Banquo'.

MURDERER 1   You made it known to us.

Macbeth persuades the murderers that they have every reason to hate Banquo. They reply that they are desperate men, willing to do anything.

87   **so gospelled**: such good Christians

89   **heavy … grave**: ill-treatment has almost killed you

90   **beggared yours**: made beggars of your children
     Liege: lord / sovereign

91   **the catalogue**: i.e. the general list of living creatures

92–3 **curs … demi-wolves**: kinds of dogs

93   **clept**: called

94   **file**: list putting them in order of value

95   **subtle**: clever

96   **housekeeper**: domestic watch-dog

97   **bounteous**: generous

98   **in him closed**: enclosed within him

99   **addition**: reputation

101 **station … file**: place in the rank order

103 **put … bosoms**: secretly reveal a plan to you

104 **takes … off**: i.e. kills your enemy

105 **Grapples … us**: makes you my closest friends

106–7 **Who … perfect**: i.e. I am in a bad way while he is alive, but would feel perfect if he were dead

109 **so … reckless**: so angered that I don't care

111 **tugged with**: knocked about by

112 **set … chance**: take any gamble with my life

113 **mend**: improve

THINK ABOUT for GCSE

Language

• What arguments does Macbeth use to persuade the murderers? What are the similarities and differences between these and the methods Lady Macbeth used on Macbeth himself in Act 1 Scene 7?

MACBETH	I did so – and went further, which is now
	Our point of second meeting. Do you find 85
	Your patience so predominant in your nature
	That you can let this go? Are you so gospelled
	To pray for this good man, and for his issue,
	Whose heavy hand hath bowed you to the grave
	And beggared yours for ever?

MURDERER 1   We are men, my Liege.   90

MACBETH   Ay, in the catalogue ye go for men –
             As hounds and greyhounds, mongrels, spaniels, curs,
             Shoughs, water-rugs, and demi-wolves are clept
             All by the name of dogs. The valued file
             Distinguishes the swift, the slow, the subtle,   95
             The housekeeper, the hunter, every one
             According to the gift which bounteous nature
             Hath in him closed – whereby he does receive
             Particular addition, from the bill
             That writes them all alike. And so of men.   100
             Now, if you have a station in the file,
             Not i' the worst rank of manhood, say it –
             And I will put that business in your bosoms,
             Whose execution takes your enemy off,
             Grapples you to the heart and love of us,   105
             Who wear our health but sickly in his life,
             Which in his death were perfect.

MURDERER 2   I am one, my Liege,
             Whom the vile blows and buffets of the world
             Have so incensed, that I am reckless what
             I do to spite the world.

MURDERER 1   And I another,   110
             So weary with disasters, tugged with fortune,
             That I would set my life on any chance
             To mend it or be rid on't.

MACBETH   Both of you
             Know Banquo was your enemy.

MURDERERS   True, my lord.

Macbeth explains to the murderers that it would be difficult for him simply to have Banquo executed because Banquo has too many friends. He commands the murderers to kill Banquo and his son Fleance that night.

115   **distance**: 1 hatred; 2 the space between two fencers

116–17 **thrusts … life**: makes a stab at my heart

118   **With … sight**: as King kill him openly

119   **bid … it**: simply say that it was my decision

121   **loves … drop**: support I cannot afford to lose
      wail his fall: grieve over the death of a man

123   **to … love**: ask for your help

124   **Masking … eye**: hiding the affair from the public

125   **sundry weighty**: a variety of very good

127   **Your … you**: i.e. I can see you're the right kind of men

129   **Acquaint … time**: let you know the best opportunity for doing the murder

131   **something**: some distance

131–2 **always … clearness**: and keeping in mind that I must remain free of suspicion

133   **rubs**: rough edges
      botches: untidy work

135   **absence … material**: death is no less important

137   **Resolve yourselves apart**: Go away and make up your minds

138   **anon**: immediately

139   **straight**: straight away
      abide within: wait inside

THINK ABOUT for GCSE

Themes and issues

• **Kingship**: Why might Macbeth be reluctant to kill Banquo himself? What does this suggest about his view of his own position as King?

Characterisation

• What impression have you formed of the murderers? Why do you think the murderers do not question the need to kill Fleance as well as Banquo?

MACBETH	So is he mine – and in such bloody distance **115**
	That every minute of his being thrusts
	Against my near'st of life. And though I could
	With bare-faced power sweep him from my sight,
	And bid my will avouch it, yet I must not,
	For certain friends, that are both his and mine, **120**
	Whose loves I may not drop, but wail his fall
	Who I myself struck down. And thence it is
	That I to your assistance do make love,
	Masking the business from the common eye,
	For sundry weighty reasons.
MURDERER 2	We shall, my lord, **125**
	Perform what you command us.
MURDERER 1	Though our lives –
MACBETH	Your spirits shine through you. Within this hour at most
	I will advise you where to plant yourselves,
	Acquaint you with the perfect spy o' the time,
	The moment on't, for 't must be done tonight **130**
	And something from the palace; always thought
	That I require a clearness. And with him
	(To leave no rubs, nor botches, in the work),
	Fleance his son, that keeps him company,
	Whose absence is no less material to me **135**
	Than is his father's, must embrace the fate
	Of that dark hour. Resolve yourselves apart:
	I'll come to you anon.
MURDERER 2	We are resolved, my lord.
MACBETH	I'll call upon you straight: abide within. –

Exeunt MURDERERS.

It is concluded. Banquo, thy soul's flight,   **140**
If it find heaven, must find it out tonight.

Exit.

In this scene ...

- Though he is now King, Macbeth is worried about the dangers which still threaten him and Lady Macbeth.
- Refusing to tell Lady Macbeth about his plan to have Banquo killed, Macbeth concludes that evil deeds need to be backed up by further crimes.

Although Macbeth and Lady Macbeth have become King and Queen as they wanted, they are not happy. Lady Macbeth tells her husband that they cannot change what has happened. But Macbeth still fears those who could be a danger to them.

THINK ABOUT for GCSE

Language

- What do the examples of antithesis (use of opposites) in lines 4 to 7 reveal about Lady Macbeth's state of mind?

Relationships

- What are the differences between Lady Macbeth's and Macbeth's feelings about their current situation?

3–4 **attend ... words**: like a few words with him if it is convenient

4 **Nought's ... spent**: We have achieved nothing and have given everything
5 **Where ... content**: when we are not happy with what we have got
7 **by ... joy**: to kill and then have our happiness ruined by worries

9 **sorriest fancies**: depressing thoughts
11–12 **Things ... regard**: i.e. If you can't put something right, don't dwell on it
13 **scorched**: gashed / wounded
14 **close ... herself**: heal up
14–15 **poor ... Remains**: feeble attempts at violence leave us
15 **former tooth**: i.e. original venom
16 **frame ... disjoint**: universe fall apart
   both the worlds: i.e. heaven and earth
17 **Ere**: before
18 **affliction**: pain / torment

20 **to peace**: i.e. to heaven
22 **restless ecstasy**: sleepless madness
23 **fitful**: restless
24 **nor ... nor ...**: neither ... nor ...

25 **Malice ... levy**: trouble at home or foreign armies

Forres: another room in the palace.

Enter LADY MACBETH, *with a* SERVANT.

LADY MACBETH   Is Banquo gone from court?

SERVANT   Ay, madam, but returns again tonight.

LADY MACBETH   Say to the King, I would attend his leisure
For a few words.

SERVANT   Madam, I will.

                                                               Exit.

LADY MACBETH   Nought's had, all's spent,
Where our desire is got without content.   5
'Tis safer to be that which we destroy
Than by destruction dwell in doubtful joy.

Enter MACBETH.

How now, my lord? Why do you keep alone,
Of sorriest fancies your companions making,
Using those thoughts which should indeed have died   10
With them they think on? Things without all remedy
Should be without regard. What's done is done.

MACBETH   We have scorched the snake, not killed it:
She'll close and be herself – whilst our poor malice
Remains in danger of her former tooth.   15
But let the frame of things disjoint, both the worlds
   suffer,
Ere we will eat our meal in fear, and sleep
In the affliction of these terrible dreams
That shake us nightly. Better be with the dead
Whom we, to gain our peace, have sent to peace,   20
Than on the torture of the mind to lie
In restless ecstasy. Duncan is in his grave.
After life's fitful fever he sleeps well.
Treason has done his worst: nor steel, nor poison,
Malice domestic, foreign levy, nothing   25
Can touch him further.

Macbeth expresses his fears about Banquo and Fleance, and hints to Lady Macbeth that something terrible is about to happen to them.

THINK ABOUT
for GCSE

Relationships

• In Act 3 Scene 1, Macbeth announced 'we will keep ourself | Till supper-time alone' (lines 42 to 43), and Lady Macbeth exited with the Lords, without speaking. Earlier in this scene she asks him 'Why do you keep alone...?' (lines 8 to 11). Here Macbeth does not tell his wife what he is planning to do. What does all this suggest about their relationship at this point? How is it different from their relationship earlier in the play?

27 **sleek o'er**: smooth over

30 **Let ... apply**: Remember to pay special attention
31 **Present him eminence**: Give him special honour
32 **Unsafe the while**: the present time is so unsafe
33 **lave our honours**: wash our achievements
34 **vizards**: masks

38 **in ... eterne**: their lives and bodies will not last for ever
39 **assailable**: open to attack
40 **jocund**: cheerful
41 **cloistered**: 1 hidden; 2 through the arches of old buildings
    Hecate: the goddess of witchcraft
42 **shard-borne**: flying on scaly wings
43 **rung ... peal**: i.e. the beetle's hum is like the tolling of the evening bell, rung when people are ready for bed
45 **chuck**: 'chick', a term of affection
46 **seeling**: blinding
47 **Scarf up**: blindfold
49 **Cancel ... pieces**: i.e. Banquo's life is like a legal document to be torn up
50 **pale**: 1 pale with fear; 2 'paled' / fenced in
    Light thickens: i.e. it becomes harder to see
53 **black agents**: evil-doers
    to ... rouse: get up and hunt
55 **Things ... ill**: Actions begun by evil are reinforced by more evil
56 **prithee**: please

LADY MACBETH	Come on,
	Gentle my lord: sleek o'er your rugged looks.
	Be bright and jovial among your guests tonight.

MACBETH So shall I, love; and so, I pray, be you.
Let your remembrance apply to Banquo.   30
Present him eminence, both with eye and tongue:
Unsafe the while, that we
Must lave our honours in these flattering streams,
And make our faces vizards to our hearts,
Disguising what they are.

LADY MACBETH   You must leave this.   35

MACBETH O, full of scorpions is my mind, dear wife!
Thou know'st that Banquo and his Fleance lives.

LADY MACBETH But in them nature's copy's not eterne.

MACBETH There's comfort yet: they are assailable.
Then be thou jocund. Ere the bat hath flown   40
His cloistered flight; ere to black Hecate's summons
The shard-borne beetle, with his drowsy hums,
Hath rung night's yawning peal, there shall be done
A deed of dreadful note.

LADY MACBETH   What's to be done?

MACBETH Be innocent of the knowledge, dearest chuck,   45
Till thou applaud the deed. Come, seeling Night,
Scarf up the tender eye of pitiful day,
And, with thy bloody and invisible hand,
Cancel and tear to pieces that great bond
Which keeps me pale! – Light thickens; and the crow   50
Makes wing to the rooky wood.
Good things of day begin to droop and drowse,
Whiles night's black agents to their preys do rouse.
Thou marvell'st at my words: but hold thee still.
Things bad begun make strong themselves by ill!   55
So, prithee, go with me.

Exeunt.

In this scene ...

• A third man joins the two murderers sent to kill Banquo and Fleance.

• They are only partly successful; although they kill Banquo, Fleance escapes.

The two murderers whose job it is to kill Banquo and Fleance are joined by a third, sent by Macbeth. They hear Banquo and Fleance approaching.

THINK ABOUT
for GCSE

Structure and form

• Who do you think the Third Murderer might be? Why might he have been sent to accompany the other two? What effect does his presence have on the opening of the scene?

---

2   **He ... mistrust**: We don't need to mistrust him

2–3 **delivers our offices**: tells us our duties

4   **To ... just**: i.e. exactly according to Macbeth's instructions

5   **yet**: still

6–7 **spurs ... inn**: the delayed traveller spurs his horse on to get to the inn on time

8   **subject ... watch**: man we are looking out for

10   **within ... expectation**: on the list of guests expected at the banquet

11   **go about**: are taking the long way round

15   **Stand to 't**: Get ready

16   **Let ... down**: wordplay – applies to both the rain and their attack

Forres: a path near the palace.

Enter three Murderers.

Murderer 1	But who did bid thee join with us?
Murderer 3	Macbeth.
Murderer 2	He needs not our mistrust, since he delivers Our offices, and what we have to do, To the direction just.
Murderer 1	Then stand with us. The west yet glimmers with some streaks of day: 5 Now spurs the lated traveller apace, To gain the timely inn; and near approaches The subject of our watch.
Murderer 3	Hark! I hear horses.
Banquo	(*Calling as he approaches*) Give us a light there, ho!
Murderer 2	Then 'tis he. The rest That are within the note of expectation 10 Already are i' the court.
Murderer 1	His horses go about.
Murderer 3	Almost a mile – but he does usually, So all men do, from hence to the palace gate Make it their walk.

Enter Banquo, *and* Fleance *with a lighted torch.*

Murderer 2	A light, a light!
Murderer 3	'Tis he.
Murderer 1	Stand to 't. 15
Banquo	(*To* Fleance) It will be rain tonight.
Murderer 1	Let it come down.

Murderers *attack.* First Murderer *strikes out Fleance's light.*

The murderers kill Banquo, but in the confusion Fleance manages to escape.

18 may'st revenge: will be able to get revenge for my death

19 Was't … way: Wasn't that the right thing to do

20 but one down: only one killed

THINK ABOUT for GCSE

Performance and staging

• Fleance manages to escape the three murderers. If you were the director, how would you make his escape seem realistic and believable?

Structure and form

• Why is it important in terms of the plot that Fleance should survive?

BANQUO O, treachery! Fly, good Fleance! Fly, fly, fly!
Thou may'st revenge – O slave!

He is cut down and killed. FLEANCE *escapes.*

MURDERER 3 Who did strike out the light?

MURDERER 1 Was't not the way?

MURDERER 3 There's but one down. The son is fled.

MURDERER 2 We have lost **20**
Best half of our affair.

MURDERER 1 Well, let's away, and say how much is done.

Exeunt.

In this scene ...

- Macbeth entertains the lords at a banquet. He is told by one of the murderers that Banquo is dead, but Fleance escaped.
- At the banquet, Macbeth sees Banquo's ghost. Despite Lady Macbeth's efforts to calm him, he cannot hide his terror, and the banquet ends abruptly.
- To find out more about the future, Macbeth decides to visit the Witches the following morning.

The banquet at Macbeth's castle begins. One of the murderers tells Macbeth in private that Banquo has been killed, but that Fleance escaped.

1 **degrees**: ranks / places
2 **at ... last**: i.e. a hearty welcome to one and all

3 **society**: the company

5 **keeps her state**: will remain seated
   in best time: at an appropriate time

7 **Pronounce it**: i.e. Tell people how welcome they are

9 **encounter**: respond to

10 **Both ... even**: There are the same number of people on each side of the table
11 **Be ... mirth**: Enjoy yourselves
   measure: toast

14 **'Tis ... within**: The blood is better on you than in him
15 **dispatched**: killed

19 **the nonpareil**: without equal

THINK ABOUT for **GCSE**

Language

- What is significant about the frequency of the word 'welcome' and its position in each speech at the beginning of the scene? Look at lines 1 to 8.

Inside the palace. A table with a banquet is set out.

Enter Macbeth *and* Lady Macbeth, *with* Ross *and* Lennox, *other* Lords, *and attendants.* Lady Macbeth *takes her seat at one end of the table.*

Macbeth	You know your own degrees, sit down: at first And last, The hearty welcome.
Lords	Thanks to your Majesty.
Macbeth	Ourself will mingle with society, And play the humble host. Our hostess keeps her state, but in best time 5 We will require her welcome.
Lady Macbeth	Pronounce it for me, sir, to all our friends – For my heart speaks, they are welcome.

Enter First Murderer *(to the doorway).*

Macbeth	(*To* Lady Macbeth) See, they encounter thee with their
	  hearts' thanks.
	(*To all at the table*) Both sides are even: here I'll sit,
	  i' the midst. 10
	Be large in mirth. Anon, we'll drink a measure
	The table round. (*Moving to talk privately with the*
	  Murderer *at the door*) There's blood upon thy face.

Murderer	'Tis Banquo's then.
Macbeth	'Tis better thee without than he within. Is he dispatched? 15
Murderer	My lord, his throat is cut: that I did for him.
Macbeth	Thou art the best o' the cut-throats. Yet he's good That did the like for Fleance: if thou didst it, Thou art the nonpareil.
Murderer	Most royal Sir, Fleance is 'scaped. 20

Macbeth is dismayed by the news that Fleance escaped. But he returns to the banquet and pretends to be disappointed at Banquo's absence from the meal. The ghost of Banquo appears in Macbeth's seat at the table.

THINK ABOUT for GCSE

Language

- What does Macbeth's language (lines 21 to 25) suggest about his state of mind? Look at his use of similes in lines 22 and 23, and the sudden shift of focus in line 25.

Performance and staging

- How would you represent Banquo's ghost in (a) a stage version; and (b) a film? Should the ghost be visible to the audience or not, in your opinion?

21 **fit**: fit of anxiety
    else: otherwise
22 **Whole ... marble**: i.e. solid as marble
    founded: secure
23 **As ... air**: as free and unrestrained as the air which surrounds us
24 **cabined, cribbed**: closed in, restricted
25 **saucy**: nagging
    safe: dealt with
26 **bides**: remains
27 **trenchèd**: cut deep like trenches
28 **The ... nature**: the smallest of which would have been enough to kill him
29 **grown serpent**: i.e. Banquo
    worm: i.e. Fleance
31 **No ... present**: i.e. Fleance is harmless for the time being
32 **hear ourselves**: discuss this

33 **give the cheer**: behave like a good host
33–5 **The feast ... welcome**: If you don't keep telling people that they are welcome, they feel as though they have paid for their meal
35 **To feed ... home**: They might as well stay at home if they just want to eat
36 **From ... ceremony**: away from home, it is courteous behaviour by the host that makes a meal special
37 **Sweet remembrancer**: i.e. Thanks for reminding me, my love
40 **country's honour**: greatest nobles
    roofed: under one roof
42 **unkindness**: bad manners
43 **mischance**: an accident
44 **Lays ... promise**: suggests he has broken his promise

MACBETH	(*Aside*) Then comes my fit again. I had else been
	    perfect –
	Whole as the marble, founded as the rock,
	As broad and general as the casing air:
	But now I am cabined, cribbed, confined, bound in
	To saucy doubts and fears. – (*To the* MURDERER) But
	    Banquo's safe?

25

MURDERER	Ay, my good lord. Safe in a ditch he bides, With twenty trenchèd gashes on his head – The least a death to nature.

MACBETH	Thanks for that. –
	(*Aside*) There the grown serpent lies: the worm, that's
	    fled,
	Hath nature that in time will venom breed –
	No teeth for the present. – (*To the* MURDERER) Get
	    thee gone. Tomorrow
	We'll hear ourselves again.

30

Exit MURDERER.

LADY MACBETH	My royal lord, You do not give the cheer. The feast is sold That is not often vouched, while 'tis a-making, 'Tis given with welcome. To feed were best at home: From thence, the sauce to meat is ceremony. Meeting were bare without it.

35

MACBETH	Sweet remembrancer! – Now, good digestion wait on appetite, And health on both!

LENNOX	May it please your Highness sit?

MACBETH	Here had we now our country's honour roofed, Were the graced person of our Banquo present –

40

Enter the GHOST OF BANQUO. *It takes Macbeth's seat at the table.*

	Who may I rather challenge for unkindness, Than pity for mischance!

ROSS	His absence, sir, Lays blame upon his promise. Please 't your Highness To grace us with your royal company?

45

Macbeth is terrified by the sight of Banquo's ghost in his seat. Lady Macbeth tries to reassure the lords, who cannot see the ghost, that her husband's strange behaviour is nothing to worry about. She privately speaks sharply to Macbeth for revealing his fear.

THINK ABOUT for GCSE

Context

• In Shakespeare's time there was some debate as to what ghosts were. Ghosts also appear in several Shakespeare plays, most often as murder victims. Why does nobody except Macbeth see the ghost?

Language

• What similarities can you see between Lady Macbeth's language here and her methods of persuasion in Act 1 Scene 7?

51 **gory locks**: bloody hair

53 **thus**: like this

55 **upon a thought**: in a moment
56 **much ... him**: you stare at him
57 **extend his passion**: prolong the fit

60 **O proper stuff**: Nonsense
61 **This ... fear**: Your fear is causing you to imagine this
63 **flaws and starts**: sudden outbursts of emotion
64 **Impostors to**: false compared with **become**: suit
66 **Authorised ... grandam**: true according to her grandmother

69 **Prithee**: I beg you

71 **charnel-houses**: bone-stores
73 **maws**: stomachs
kites: birds that feed off the flesh of dead animals

MACBETH	The table's full.
LENNOX	Here is a place reserved, sir.
MACBETH	Where?
LENNOX	Here, my good lord. (**MACBETH** *sees the* **GHOST**.) What is't that moves your Highness?
MACBETH	Which of you have done this?
LORDS	What, my good lord?
MACBETH	(*To the* **GHOST**) Thou canst not say I did it! Never shake 50 Thy gory locks at me!
ROSS	Gentlemen, rise: his Highness is not well.
LADY MACBETH	Sit, worthy friends. My lord is often thus, And hath been from his youth. Pray you, keep seat. The fit is momentary: upon a thought 55 He will again be well. If much you note him You shall offend him, and extend his passion. (*Rising from the table*) Feed, and regard him not. – (*Aside to* **MACBETH**) Are you a man?
MACBETH	Ay, and a bold one, that dare look on that Which might appal the devil.
LADY MACBETH	O proper stuff! 60 This is the very painting of your fear: This is the air-drawn dagger which, you said, Led you to Duncan. O! – these flaws and starts (Impostors to true fear) would well become A woman's story at a winter's fire, 65 Authorised by her grandam. Shame itself! Why do you make such faces? When all's done, You look but on a stool.
MACBETH	Prithee, see there! Behold! Look! Lo! – how say you? Why – what care I? (*To the* **GHOST**) If thou canst nod, speak too! – 70 If charnel-houses and our graves must send Those that we bury back, our monuments Shall be the maws of kites!

Exit **GHOST**.

Macbeth apologises to the lords and tries to regain his calmness, but is again terrified when the ghost reappears.

THINK ABOUT
for GCSE

Performance and staging

- What is it about the appearance and behaviour of Banquo's ghost that Macbeth finds particularly terrifying? Look at Macbeth's reaction in lines 49 to 51, 69 to 73, 75 to 83, and 93 to 96. How can these aspects of the ghost be made frightening on stage?

- What do you think the Lords are making of Macbeth's behaviour and the reason he gives for it? Look at lines 84 to 87. If you were directing the play, what would you tell the Lords to do in reaction to Macbeth's strange behaviour?

73 **Quite ... folly**: Has your foolishness made you lose your manhood completely

75 **ere**: before
76 **humane ... weal**: human laws cleansed society and made it civilised

79 **when ... out**: when a man had had his brains bashed out
81 **mortal ... crowns**: fatal wounds on their heads

84 **do lack you**: are missing your company

85 **muse**: be surprised
86 **infirmity**: weakness

92 **all to all**: Good health to everyone

pledge: toast

93 **Avaunt**: Be gone

95 **Thou ... eyes**: there is no sign of life in your eyes

97 **a thing of custom**: nothing out of the ordinary

LADY MACBETH	What! Quite unmanned in folly?
MACBETH	If I stand here, I saw him!
LADY MACBETH	Fie! – for shame!

MACBETH   Blood hath been shed ere now, i' the olden time,   **75**
Ere humane statute purged the gentle weal –
Ay, and since too, murders have been performed
Too terrible for the ear. The time has been
That, when the brains were out, the man would die,
And there an end. But now they rise again   **80**
With twenty mortal murders on their crowns,
And push us from our stools. This is more strange
Than such a murder is.

LADY MACBETH   My worthy lord,
Your noble friends do lack you.

MACBETH   I do forget. –
(*To the* LORDS) Do not muse at me, my most worthy
   friends.   **85**
I have a strange infirmity, which is nothing
To those that know me. Come, love and health to all.
Then I'll sit down. – Give me some wine: fill full. –
I drink to the general joy o' the whole table –
And to our dear friend Banquo, whom we miss.   **90**
Would he were here.

    Re-enter the GHOST.

    To all, and him, we thirst –
And all to all.

LORDS   Our duties – and the pledge.

MACBETH   (*To the* GHOST) Avaunt and quit my sight! Let the earth
   hide thee!
Thy bones are marrowless, thy blood is cold –
Thou hast no speculation in those eyes   **95**
Which thou dost glare with!

LADY MACBETH   (*To the* LORDS) Think of this, good peers,
But as a thing of custom: 'tis no other –
Only it spoils the pleasure of the time.

105

Unable to control her husband's strange behaviour, Lady Macbeth eventually tells the lords to leave.

101   **Hyrcan**: from Hyrcania, wild country by the Caspian Sea

102   **but *that***: i.e. except Banquo's

104   **dare ... desert**: i.e. to a fight to the death, with no-one around to interrupt

105–6   **If ... girl**: If I fear and tremble then, you can call me a feeble creature

109   **displaced the mirth**: ruined the good mood of the feast

110   **most admired disorder**: this amazing fit of madness

112–6   **You ... fear**: i.e. I always thought I was brave; but I am amazed to see you unmoved by such sights

116   **blanched**: turned white

119   **Stand ... going**: Don't worry about leaving in order of rank

122   **It will ... blood**: i.e. murder will lead to more bloodshed or execution

---

THINK ABOUT *for* GCSE

Themes and issues

• **Order** and disorder are important in this play. How is disorder represented in this part of the scene? Look at Lady Macbeth's speeches in lines 109 to 110, and 117 to 120.

• Lady Macbeth has taunted Macbeth with being 'unmanned' (line 73). What seems to be their definition of '**manhood**'? Look, for example, at lines 99 to 106, and 112 to 116.

MACBETH   What man dare, I dare!
            Approach thou like the rugged Russian bear,   100
            The armed rhinoceros, or the Hyrcan tiger –
            Take any shape but *that*, and my firm nerves
            Shall never tremble. Or be alive again,
            And dare me to the desert with thy sword –
            If trembling I inhabit then, protest me   105
            The baby of a girl! Hence horrible shadow! –
            Unreal mockery! Hence! –

                                    Exit GHOST.

                        Why, so. – Being gone,
            I am a man again. – (*To the* LORDS) Pray you, sit still.

LADY MACBETH (*To* MACBETH) You have displaced the mirth, broke
                 the good meeting,
              With most admired disorder.

MACBETH   Can such things be,   110
            And overcome us like a summer's cloud,
            Without our special wonder? You make me strange
            Even to the disposition that I owe,
            When now I think you can behold such sights
            And keep the natural ruby of your cheeks,   115
            When mine is blanched with fear.

ROSS   What sights, my lord?

LADY MACBETH (*To the* LORDS) I pray you, speak not: he grows worse
                 and worse.
              Question enrages him. At once, good night. –
              Stand not upon the order of your going,
              But go at once.

LENNOX   Good night, and better health   120
           Attend his Majesty!

LADY MACBETH   A kind good night to all.

          Exit LENNOX, **with** ROSS, **other** LORDS **and attendants.**

MACBETH   It will have blood, they say, blood will have blood.

Macbeth thinks about the many ways in which murders come to light. He finds it suspicious that Macduff refused to attend that night's banquet and decides to visit the Witches again the next morning. He now knows that he will have to commit further bloody deeds.

THINK ABOUT for GCSE

Characterisation

• What does Macbeth say which shows that he is (a) superstitious; (b) suspicious of his lords; and (c) prepared to commit more violence? Look at lines 122 onwards.

Context

• What does Macbeth say here which reminds us that it was not unknown in Shakespeare's time for households to contain spies in the pay of the monarch or some powerful lord?

Relationships

• In one production, Macbeth and Lady Macbeth exited at the end of the scene to different bedrooms. What is your impression of their relationship at this point? How might you show this in performance?

124 **Augurs ... relations**: Prophecies and knowledge about how events are linked

125 **maggot-pies ... rooks**: birds used as omens

125–6 **brought ... blood**: exposed the most hidden murderers

127 **Almost ... which**: i.e. Night is arguing with morning about which it is

128 **denies his person**: refuses to be present

130 **by the way**: on the grapevine

132 **fee'd**: paid by me (as a spy)

133 **betimes**: very early

134 **bent**: determined

135 **the worst means**: the most evil methods (i.e. witchcraft)

135–6 **For mine ... way**: I will sacrifice everything else to get what I want

138 **go o'er**: crossing to the other side

139 **will to hand**: must be put into practice

140 **acted ... scanned**: i.e. acted upon before I think too much about them

141 **season**: preservative, i.e. what keeps us fresh

142 **self-abuse**: self-deception (imagining Banquo's ghost)

143 **initiate**: beginner's

144 **young in deed**: i.e. new to crimes like this

	Stones have been known to move, and trees to speak.	
	Augurs, and understood relations, have	
	By maggot-pies and choughs, and rooks, brought forth	**125**
	The secret'st man of blood. What is the night?	
LADY MACBETH	Almost at odds with morning, which is which.	
MACBETH	How say'st thou, that Macduff denies his person	
	At our great bidding?	
LADY MACBETH	Did you send to him, sir?	
MACBETH	I hear it by the way: but I will send.	**130**
	There's not a one of them, but in his house	
	I keep a servant fee'd. I will tomorrow –	
	And betimes I will – to the weird sisters.	
	More shall they speak – for now I am bent to know	
	By the worst means, the worst. For mine own good	**135**
	All causes shall give way. I am in blood	
	Stepped in so far, that, should I wade no more,	
	Returning were as tedious as go o'er.	
	Strange things I have in head, that will to hand,	
	Which must be acted ere they may be scanned.	**140**
LADY MACBETH	You lack the season of all natures, sleep.	
MACBETH	Come, we'll to sleep. My strange and self-abuse	
	Is the initiate fear, that wants hard use.	
	We are yet but young in deed.	

Exeunt.

In this scene ...

- The Witches are visited by the Witch goddess Hecate, who is angry about the way they have dealt with Macbeth.

The Witch goddess Hecate is angry that the Witches have not involved her in their dealings with Macbeth. She vows to lead Macbeth to his destruction.

THINK ABOUT for GCSE

Context

- King James's book, *Demonologie*, described witches' powers. They included: predicting the future, defying normal physical laws, affecting the weather, cursing enemies and using 'familiar' spirits in the shape of animals. Where has each of these powers been in evidence in *Macbeth*?

Structure and form

- What does Hecate's speech suggest about Macbeth's ultimate fate?

2 **beldams**: hags
3 **Saucy**: impertinent
4 **traffic**: have dealings

7 **close contriver**: secret plotter
8 **bear my part**: take part

11 **wayward son**: unreliable follower
12 **wrathful**: angry
13 **Loves ... ends**: loves witchcraft purely for what he can get out of it
15 **Acheron**: One of the rivers of the underworld, in classical mythology.
16 **Thither**: There
21 **Unto ... end**: planning something ruinous and deadly
24 **vaporous drop**: People believed that the moon shed drops of powerful foam onto certain plants which could then be used in witches' spells.
    profound: ready to fall
26 **distilled**: i.e. turned into something powerful
    sleights: tricks
27 **artificial sprites**: spirits raised by magic
28 **illusion**: power to deceive
29 **confusion**: destruction
30 **spurn**: think nothing of
30–1 **bear ... 'bove**: have unrealistic hopes and be blind to
32 **security**: over-confidence
33 **mortals**: i.e. ordinary humans

Thunder.

Enter the three Witches, *meeting* Hecate (*the Witch goddess*).

Witch 1	Why, how now, Hecate? You look angerly.
Hecate	Have I not reason, beldams as you are,
	Saucy, and overbold? How did you dare
	To trade and traffic with Macbeth,
	In riddles, and affairs of death?

Have I not reason, beldams as you are,
Saucy, and overbold? How did you dare
To trade and traffic with Macbeth,
In riddles, and affairs of death?   5
And I, the mistress of your charms,
The close contriver of all harms,
Was never called to bear my part,
Or show the glory of our art?
And, which is worse, all you have done   10
Hath been but for a wayward son,
Spiteful and wrathful – who, as others do,
Loves for his own ends, not for you.
But make amends now. Get you gone,
And at the pit of Acheron   15
Meet me i' the morning. Thither he
Will come to know his destiny.
Your vessels and your spells provide,
Your charms, and everything beside.
I am for the air. This night I'll spend   20
Unto a dismal and a fatal end.
Great business must be wrought ere noon.
Upon the corner of the moon
There hangs a vaporous drop profound.
I'll catch it ere it come to ground –   25
And that, distilled by magic sleights,
Shall raise such artificial sprites,
As, by the strength of their illusion,
Shall draw him on to his confusion.
He shall spurn fate, scorn death, and bear   30
His hopes 'bove wisdom, grace and fear.
And you all know, security
Is mortals' chiefest enemy.

Hecate is called away.

35   **stays**: waits

THINK ABOUT for GCSE

Performance and staging

- This scene is often cut in performance. Why might some directors decide to cut it?

Structure and form

- If it is included, what does it add in terms of (a) the plot; (b) the supernatural atmosphere; (c) our understanding of Macbeth; and (d) our understanding of the Witches and their motives?

Music and singing heard in the distance ('Come away, come away, Hecate, Hecate, come away! ...').

    Hark! I am called. My little spirit, see,
    Sits in a foggy cloud, and stays for me.   **35**

                                   Exit.

WITCH 1   Come, let's make haste! She'll soon be back again.

                             Exeunt.

In this scene ...

- Lennox talks about Macbeth's murderous behaviour with another lord.
- The lord tells Lennox that Malcolm has fled to England and that Macduff has gone there to seek support for an attempt to overthrow Macbeth.

Lennox tells another lord that he is suspicious about the deaths of Duncan and Banquo. The lord reports that Malcolm is with the English King, Edward the Confessor, and that Macduff has gone there hoping to find support for an attack on Macbeth.

THINK ABOUT for GCSE

Performance and staging

- In what tone should an actor playing Lennox speak lines 3 to 20? Think about the difference between what he says and what he really means.

1 **My former speeches**: What I have already said

  but ... thoughts: simply matches what you have been thinking

2 **Which ... farther**: it's up to you to draw your own conclusions

3 **Things ... borne**: mysterious things have happened

4 **of**: by

8 **want the thought**: help thinking

10 **fact**: crime

11 **straight**: straightaway

12 **pious**: loyal

  delinquents: i.e. Duncan's two attendants

13 **thralls**: prisoners

17 **borne**: managed

18 **under his key**: in prison

19 **an't**: if it

21 **from broad words**: because of his outspoken comments

22 **tyrant**: i.e. Macbeth

24 **bestows himself**: is staying

25 **due of birth**: i.e. crown which is rightfully his

28 **malevolence of fortune**: i.e. loss of Malcolm's throne

28–9 **nothing ... respect**: has not meant that he has received less respect

29 **Thither**: There, i.e. to England

30 **pray**: ask

  upon his aid: on Malcolm's behalf

31 **wake**: rouse up

Forres: the edge of the town.

Enter LENNOX, *with another* LORD.

LENNOX	My former speeches have but hit your thoughts,
	Which can interpret farther. Only, I say,
	Things have been strangely borne. The gracious Duncan
	Was pitied of Macbeth. Marry, he was dead.
	And the right-valiant Banquo walked too late – 5
	Whom you may say, if 't please you, Fleance killed,
	For Fleance fled. Men must not walk too late.
	Who cannot want the thought how monstrous
	It was for Malcolm and for Donalbain
	To kill their gracious father? Damnèd fact! 10
	How it did grieve Macbeth! Did he not straight,
	In pious rage, the two delinquents tear,
	That were the slaves of drink, and thralls of sleep?
	Was not that nobly done? Ay, and wisely, too.
	For 'twould have angered any heart alive 15
	To hear the men deny 't. So that, I say,
	He has borne all things well. And I do think
	That, had he Duncan's sons under his key –
	As, an't please Heaven, he shall not – they should find
	What 'twere to kill a father. So should Fleance. 20
	But, peace! – For from broad words, and 'cause he failed
	His presence at the tyrant's feast, I hear
	Macduff lives in disgrace. Sir, can you tell
	Where he bestows himself?
LORD	The son of Duncan,
	From whom this tyrant holds the due of birth, 25
	Lives in the English court – and is received
	Of the most pious Edward with such grace,
	That the malevolence of fortune nothing
	Takes from his high respect. Thither Macduff
	Is gone to pray the holy King, upon his aid, 30
	To wake Northumberland, and warlike Siward –

Lennox and the lord agree that Macduff would be well advised to stay out of Macbeth's way.

32 Him above: God
33 ratify: support

36 Do ... honours: show our loyal duty to the King and be honestly rewarded
37 pine: painfully long
38 exasperate: angered

41 cloudy: scowling (at Macduff's refusal to submit)
42–3 rue ... answer: come to regret that you answered me like this

44 Advise ... caution: warn Macduff to be careful
44–5 hold ... provide: keep a sensible distance from Macbeth

49 accursed: i.e. wicked

THINK ABOUT *for* GCSE

Structure and form

• What are the main purposes of this scene in performance – apart from giving the actor playing Macbeth a rest? Think about what information it conveys, which new characters who might become important later are referred to, and what it tells us about the situation in Scotland.

Language

• Look at the final speeches by Lennox and the lord (lines 45 to 49). How does the language reflect their feelings that the forces against Macbeth are holy, while Macbeth himself is damned?

That, by the help of these (with Him above
To ratify the work), we may again
Give to our tables meat, sleep to our nights,
Free from our feasts and banquets bloody knives,   35
Do faithful homage, and receive free honours –
All which we pine for now. And this report
Hath so exasperate the King that he
Prepares for some attempt of war.

LENNOX   Sent he to Macduff?

LORD   He did. And with an absolute 'Sir, not I,'   40
The cloudy messenger turns me his back,
And hums, as who should say, 'You'll rue the time
That clogs me with this answer.'

LENNOX   And that well might
Advise him to a caution, to hold what distance
His wisdom can provide. Some holy angel   45
Fly to the court of England and unfold
His message ere he come – that a swift blessing
May soon return to this our suffering country
Under a hand accursed!

LORD   I'll send my prayers with him.

Exeunt.

In this scene ...

- Macbeth visits the Witches and is shown a series of mysterious visions about what will happen in the future.
- As the Witches disappear, Lennox arrives to report that Macduff has gone to England.
- Macbeth instantly decides to kill everyone in Macduff's castle.

The Witches prepare for their meeting with Macbeth by creating a powerful magic potion.

THINK ABOUT for GCSE

Performance and staging

- What would be an effective setting for this scene (a) on stage; and (b) in a film?
- The Witches use 'Liver of blaspheming Jew' (line 26). In Shakespeare's time there was an irrational hatred of Jews. If you were a director, how would you reply to an actor who said 'I'm not saying that line – it's anti-Semitic'?

1 **brindled**: tabby

2 **hedge-pig**: hedgehog

3 **Harpier**: the third Witch's attendant spirit

5 **entrails**: animals' insides

8 **Sweltered venom**: has been sweating out poison
sleeping got: taken while sleeping

12 **Fillet**: A thin slice
fenny: found in bogs and marshes

16 **fork**: forked tongue
blind-worm: slow-worm (a harmless snake-like lizard)

17 **howlet**: young owl

23 **Witches' mummy**: a medicinal powder made from Egyptian mummies
maw and gulf: stomach and throat

24 **ravined ... shark**: a shark that has eaten its fill

25 **hemlock**: a poisonous plant

26 **blaspheming**: speaking against God

27 **Gall**: bitter fluid from the liver
slips: cuttings

28 **Slivered**: sliced off

29–30 **Turk ... Tartar ... birth-strangled babe**: Like the Jew, all would be attractive to the Witches because they were not christened.

A shadowy cavern: a steaming cauldron at its centre.

Thunder.

Enter the three WITCHES.

WITCH 1	Thrice the brindled cat hath mewed.	
WITCH 2	Thrice and once the hedge-pig whined.	
WITCH 3	Harpier cries – 'tis time, 'tis time!	
WITCH 1	Round about the cauldron go –	
	In the poisoned entrails throw.	5
	Toad, that under cold stone	
	Days and nights has thirty-one	
	Sweltered venom, sleeping got,	
	Boil thou first i' the charmèd pot.	
ALL	Double, double, toil and trouble –	
	Fire burn and cauldron bubble!	10
WITCH 2	Fillet of a fenny snake,	
	In the cauldron boil and bake –	
	Eye of newt, and toe of frog,	
	Wool of bat and tongue of dog,	15
	Adder's fork, and blind-worm's sting,	
	Lizard's leg, and howlet's wing –	
	For a charm of powerful trouble,	
	Like a hell-broth boil and bubble.	
ALL	Double, double, toil and trouble –	20
	Fire burn and cauldron bubble!	
WITCH 3	Scale of dragon, tooth of wolf,	
	Witches' mummy, maw and gulf	
	Of the ravined salt-sea shark,	
	Root of hemlock digged i' the dark;	25
	Liver of blaspheming Jew,	
	Gall of goat, and slips of yew	
	Slivered in the moon's eclipse;	
	Nose of Turk, and Tartar's lips;	

Hecate enters with three more Witches. Macbeth arrives and commands the Witches to answer his questions, whatever the consequences.

31 drab: prostitute
32 slab: sticky
33 chawdron: insides

39 commend your pains: congratulate you on your efforts

44 pricking ... thumbs: People believed that sudden pains were a sign that something was about to happen.

THINK ABOUT for GCSE

Themes and issues

- Which speech here picks up the important theme of **order and nature**? What form does the disorder take?

Language

- Look at the form of verse in which the Witches speak here and find examples of internal rhyme and a four-beat rhythm. Why is this sort of verse suited to the uttering of spells?

50 conjure: call upon
profess: practise, i.e. witchcraft
52–3 untie ... churches: i.e. cause the wind to knock churches down
53 yeasty: foaming
54 Confound ... up: confuse and overwhelm ships
55 bladed ... lodged: unripe corn be blown flat
57 slope: bend / collapse

	Finger of birth-strangled babe,	30
	Ditch-delivered by a drab –	
	Make the gruel thick and slab.	
	Add thereto a tiger's chawdron,	
	For th' ingredients of our cauldron.	

ALL   Double, double, toil and trouble –   35
             Fire burn and cauldron bubble!

WITCH 2 Cool it with a baboon's blood –
             Then the charm is firm and good.

Enter HECATE, *with three more Witches.*

HECATE   O well done! I commend your pains,
             And every one shall share i' the gains.   40
             And now about the cauldron sing,
             Like elves and fairies in a ring,
             Enchanting all that you put in.

Music. All the WITCHES *join in a wild dance round the cauldron
and sing – 'Black spirits and white, red spirits and grey,
Mingle, mingle ...'.*

Exit HECATE, *with the Witches who came with her.*

WITCH 2 By the pricking of my thumbs
             Something wicked this way comes! –   45
             Open, locks –
             Whoever knocks.

Enter MACBETH.

MACBETH How now, you secret, black and midnight hags!
             What is't you do?

ALL   A deed without a name.

MACBETH I conjure you by that which you profess,   50
             Howe'er you come to know it, answer me.
             Though you untie the winds and let them fight
             Against the churches, though the yeasty waves
             Confound and swallow navigation up –
             Though bladed corn be lodged and trees blown down,   55
             Though castles topple on their warders' heads,
             Though palaces and pyramids do slope

The Witches summon apparitions to give Macbeth the answers he wants. An armoured head warns Macbeth to beware of Macduff. Next a blood-stained child appears.

59 **nature's germens**: the seeds of creation
60 **sicken**: i.e. is sick (with over-eating)

63 **our masters**: the spirits that the Witches serve

65 **nine farrow**: litter of nine piglets
65–6 **Grease … gibbet**: Sweat, that's dripped from a murderer who has been hanged

68 **office**: your function (to appear and foretell what will happen)
    deftly: skilfully

THINK ABOUT for GCSE

Performance and staging

• There is some argument about what the 'armoured head' represents. Some people think that it is Macbeth's own head, cut off by Macduff; others that it is Macduff himself. What do you think? Could it represent anything else?

74 **harped**: guessed
    aright: correctly

76 **potent**: powerful

s.d. **a bloodstained child**: representing Macduff, 'untimely ripped' from his mother's womb (see Act 5 Scene 8, lines 15 to 16)

	Their heads to their foundations – though the treasure	
	Of nature's germens tumble all together	
	Even till destruction sicken! – answer me	60
	To what I ask you.	

WITCH 1   Speak.

WITCH 2   Demand.

WITCH 3   We'll answer.

WITCH 1   Say, if thou'dst rather hear it from our mouths,
            Or from our masters.

MACBETH   Call 'em. Let me see 'em.

WITCH 1   Pour in sow's blood, that hath eaten
            Her nine farrow. Grease, that's sweaten   65
            From the murderer's gibbet, throw
            Into the flame.

ALL   Come, high or low! –
            Thyself and office deftly show.

Thunder.
First APPARITION *– **an armoured head** – rises above the cauldron.*

MACBETH   Tell me, thou unknown power, –

WITCH 1   He knows thy thought.
            Hear his speech, but say thou nought.   70

APPARITION 1 Macbeth! Macbeth! Macbeth! Beware Macduff!
              Beware the Thane of Fife! Dismiss me. – Enough.

                               APPARITION *sinks from sight.*

MACBETH   Whate'er thou art, for thy good caution, thanks:
            Thou hast harped my fear aright. But one word more –

WITCH 1   He will not be commanded. Here's another,   75
            More potent than the first.

Thunder.
Second APPARITION *– **a bloodstained child** – rises.*

APPARITION 2 Macbeth! Macbeth! Macbeth! –

MACBETH   Had I three ears, I'd hear thee!

The second apparition tells Macbeth that he can't be harmed by a man born of a woman. Despite this reassurance, Macbeth vows to kill Macduff. A third apparition tells Macbeth that he cannot be defeated until Birnam Wood comes to his castle. Macbeth then asks whether Banquo's descendants will ever be kings of Scotland.

THINK ABOUT for GCSE

Structure and form

• Think about what each of the three apparitions might represent. Why do you think the Witches are showing them to Macbeth? To help him? To lead him to destruction?

Characterisation

• How would you describe Macbeth's attitude to the apparitions? Why do you think he responds in this way?

Themes and issues

• How do the witches' prophecies (lines 79 to 81, and 90 to 94) add to our understanding of **equivocation** as it is represented in this play?

80 **none ... born**: no man that a woman has given birth to

83 **make ... sure**: make doubly sure (by killing Macduff anyway, even though he supposedly cannot be harmed by him)

84 **take ... fate**: i.e. make Fate stick to its contract

s.d. **a child ... hand**: representing Malcolm, the true King, with a tree from Birnam Wood (see Act 5 Scene 4, lines 4 to 7)

87 **issue**: descendant / child

88–9 **round ... sovereignty**: i.e. the crown

90 **lion-mettled**: courageous as a lion

91 **chafes**: is angry
    frets: complains

92 **vanquished**: defeated

95 **impress the forest**: make the forest join an army

96 **bodements**: predictions

97 **Rebellious dead**: Those who have been killed for opposing Macbeth

99 **lease of nature**: full natural life-span

99–100 **pay ... custom**: die in the normal way (as if paying a debt)

101 **art**: skill (of witchcraft)

APPARITION 2	Be bloody, bold and resolute! Laugh to scorn
	The power of man – for none of woman born **80**
	Shall harm Macbeth.

*APPARITION **sinks away.***

MACBETH	Then live, Macduff. What need I fear of thee?
	But yet I'll make assurance double sure,
	And take a bond of fate: thou shalt not live! –
	That I may tell pale-hearted fear it lies, **85**
	And sleep in spite of thunder. –

Thunder.
*Third APPARITION – **a child wearing a crown, with a small
green tree in his hand** – rises.*

What is this,
That rises like the issue of a king,
And wears upon his baby brow the round
And top of sovereignty?

ALL	Listen – but speak not to it.

APPARITION 3	Be lion-mettled, proud, and take no care **90**
	Who chafes, who frets, or where conspirers are!
	Macbeth shall never vanquished be, until
	Great Birnam wood to high Dunsinane hill
	Shall come against him.

*APPARITION **sinks away.***

MACBETH	That will never be!
	Who can impress the forest? Bid the tree **95**
	Unfix his earth-bound root? Sweet bodements! Good!
	Rebellious dead, rise never, till the wood
	Of Birnam rise – and our high-placed Macbeth
	Shall live the lease of nature, pay his breath
	To time and mortal custom. – Yet my heart **100**
	Throbs to know one thing. Tell me (if your art
	Can tell so much), shall Banquo's issue ever
	Reign in this kingdom?

ALL	Seek to know no more.

MACBETH	I will be satisfied! Deny me this,
	And an eternal curse fall on you! Let me know. – **105**

The Witches show Macbeth
a procession of eight Kings,
accompanied by the ghost of
Banquo himself. Macbeth is
shocked to realise that the Kings
are Banquo's descendants.

THINK ABOUT
for GCSE

Performance and staging

• How would you represent
the three apparitions and
the show of Kings (a) on
stage; and (b) in a film?

• What are the advantages
and disadvantages of having
the Witches played by men,
as they would have been
in Shakespeare's time and
sometimes are now?

Context

• It is possible that
King James was in the
audience of at least one
performance of *Macbeth*.
Why might he have been
particularly interested in
the presentation of the
procession of kings?

s.d. **a procession ... mirror**: a silent
procession of eight Kings, descended
from Banquo (who are also the
ancestors of James I)

113 **sear**: scorch

116 **Start**: Jump from your sockets
crack of doom: dawning of the day of
Judgement
119 **glass**: mirror

121 **two-fold ... sceptres**: These represent
the orbs carried in the double
coronation of King James in Scotland
and England; the treble sceptres are
the two used in the English coronation
and one in the Scottish.
123 **blood-boltered**: with hair clotted with
blood
124 **for his**: claiming them as his
descendants
127 **sprites**: spirits

130 **antic round**: i.e. a strange, grotesque
dance
132 **Our ... pay**: we treated him well and
made it worth his while coming here

Eerie music (oboes): the Witches' cauldron begins to sink away.

Why sinks that cauldron? And what noise is this?

WITCH 1   Show!

WITCH 2   Show!

WITCH 3   Show!

ALL   Show his eyes, and grieve his heart!   110
Come like shadows – so depart.

Enter a procession of eight phantom KINGS, the last of them carrying a mirror. The GHOST of BANQUO follows them.

MACBETH   (*To the first KING*) Thou art too like the spirit of
  Banquo! Down!
Thy crown does sear mine eye-balls! (*To the second*)
  And thy hair,
Thou other gold-bound brow, is like the first.
A third is like the former. – Filthy hags! –   115
Why do you show me this? – A fourth? – Start, eyes!
What! – Will the line stretch out t' the crack of doom?
Another yet? – A seventh? – I'll see no more! –
And yet the eighth appears, who bears a glass
Which shows me many more. And some I see   120
That two-fold balls and treble sceptres carry.
Horrible sight! – Now, I see 'tis true –
For the blood-boltered Banquo smiles upon me,
And points at them for his. – What! Is this so?

WITCH 1   Ay, sir, all this is so.

Phantom KINGS and GHOST disappear.

  – But why   125
Stands Macbeth thus amazèdly?
Come, sisters, cheer we up his sprites,
And show the best of our delights.
I'll charm the air to give a sound,
While you perform your antic round –   130
That this great King may kindly say,
Our duties did his welcome pay.

The Witches vanish. Lennox arrives to report that Macduff has fled to England. Macbeth decides to attack Macduff's castle and to kill his family.

133   **pernicious**: harmful
134   **Stand aye accursèd**: be forever cursed
135   **without there**: you outside

THINK ABOUT for GCSE

Characterisation

- How far do you think each of these adjectives describes Macbeth at this point in the play: courageous, impulsive, violent, cowardly, superstitious, intelligent, deceitful, practical, and frightened?

- What do we learn from his final speech (lines 144 to 156) about his state of mind at this stage in the play? How do you react to his resolution and plan of action?

144   **thou ... exploits**: you are one step ahead of my terrible actions
145–6   **The flighty ... it**: i.e. unless you perform a deed the moment you think of it, it is too late
147–8   **The very ... hand**: I will act as soon as I think
149   **crown my thoughts**: round off
150   **surprise**: attack suddenly
151   **give ... sword**: i.e. kill
153   **That ... line**: i.e. his descendants
154   **before ... cool**: while I am still fired up to do it

Music. The WITCHES *circle in a wild dance, then vanish.*

MACBETH	Where are they? Gone? – Let this pernicious hour Stand aye accursèd in the calendar! – Come in, without there!

Enter LENNOX.

LENNOX	What's your Grace's will?	**135**
MACBETH	Saw you the weird sisters?	
LENNOX	No, my lord.	
MACBETH	Came they not by you?	
LENNOX	No, indeed, my lord.	
MACBETH	Infected be the air whereon they ride – And damned all those that trust them! – I did hear The galloping of horse. Who was't came by?	**140**
LENNOX	'Tis two or three, my lord, that bring you word Macduff is fled to England.	
MACBETH	Fled to England?	
LENNOX	Ay, my good lord.	
MACBETH	(*Aside*) Time, thou anticipat'st my dread exploits: The flighty purpose never is o'ertook, Unless the deed go with it. From this moment The very firstlings of my heart shall be The firstlings of my hand. And even now, To crown my thoughts with acts, be it thought and done. The castle of Macduff I will surprise: Seize upon Fife – give to the edge o' the sword His wife, his babes, and all unfortunate souls That trace him in his line. No boasting, like a fool – This deed I'll do before this purpose cool! But no more sights! – (*To* LENNOX) Where are these gentlemen? Come, bring me where they are.	**145** **150** **155**

Exeunt.

In this scene ...

- Ross visits Lady Macduff. She cannot understand why her husband has left her to flee to England.
- After Ross leaves, a frightened messenger urges Lady Macduff to escape from the approaching danger.
- Murderers kill Lady Macduff's son and chase her as she tries to escape.

In Macduff's castle, Lady Macduff tells Ross that her husband showed little thought for his family when he fled to England. Ross tries to explain the reason for Macduff's actions.

3–4 **When ... traitors**: i.e. Even though Macduff was not a traitor, running away made him look like one

7 **titles**: lands and possessions owned as Thane of Fife

9 **wants ... touch**: i.e. lacks the normal feelings of a father and husband

12 **All ... love**: His actions are motivated totally by fear, not by love for his family

14 **runs ... reason**: goes against common sense
coz: cousin (or any close relative)

15 **school yourself**: learn to live with it / control yourself

16 **judicious**: possesses sound judgement

17 **The ... season**: the way things violently change these days

19 **And ... ourselves**: without realising it
hold rumour: believe rumours

22 **Each ... move**: and are swept this way and that

24 **climb upward**: get better

THINK ABOUT for GCSE

Performance and staging

- In the Roman Polanski film, Ross was portrayed as deceitful and treacherous, but in most productions he is loyal and honest. If you were the director, how would you want him to be played?

Fife: inside Macduff's castle.

Enter LADY MACDUFF, *and her young* SON, *with* ROSS.

LADY MACDUFF What had he done, to make him fly the land?

ROSS You must have patience, madam.

LADY MACDUFF   *He* had none:
His flight was madness. When our actions do not,
Our fears do make us traitors.

ROSS   You know not
Whether it was his wisdom or his fear.   5

LADY MACDUFF Wisdom! – to leave his wife, to leave his babes,
His mansion and his titles, in a place
From whence himself does fly? He loves us not.
He wants the natural touch – for the poor wren,
The most diminutive of birds, will fight,   10
Her young ones in her nest, against the owl.
All is the fear, and nothing is the love;
As little is the wisdom, where the flight
So runs against all reason.

ROSS   My dearest coz,
I pray you, school yourself. But for your husband,   10
He is noble, wise, judicious, and best knows
The fits o' the season. I dare not speak much further:
But cruel are the times, when we are traitors,
And do not know ourselves – when we hold rumour
From what we fear, yet know not what we fear,   20
But float upon a wild and violent sea
Each way, and move. – I take my leave of you:
Shall not be long but I'll be here again.
Things at the worst will cease, or else climb upward
To what they were before. – (*To the* SON) My pretty
    cousin,   25
Blessing upon you!

LADY MACDUFF Fathered he is, and yet he's fatherless.

When Ross leaves, Lady Macduff tells her son that his father is dead, but the boy refuses to believe her.

29 **It ... discomfort**: i.e. I fear I will start to weep

30 **Sirrah**: i.e. Boy

34 **lime**: sticky substance for trapping birds
35 **pit-fall**: covered hole / trap
   gin: snare
36 **Poor ... for**: i.e. They are only set for rich and powerful people

---

THINK ABOUT for **GCSE**

Relationships

• What does the conversation between Lady Macbeth and her son reveal about their relationship, and the relationship between Lady Macduff and her husband?

Structure and form

• Why is it important for us to see Lady Macduff and her son before the murderers arrive?

---

42 **wit**: intelligence
43 **And ... thee**: it isn't much, but it's not bad for a child of your age

47 **swears and lies**: takes an oath and breaks it
48 **be ... so**: are all people who do that traitors

ROSS	I am so much a fool, should I stay longer,
	It would be my disgrace and your discomfort.
	I take my leave at once.

Exit.

| LADY MACDUFF | Sirrah, your father's dead: | 30 |
| | And what will you do now? How will you live? |

| SON | As birds do, mother. |

| LADY MACDUFF | What, with worms and flies? |

| SON | With what I get, I mean – and so do they. |

| LADY MACDUFF | Poor bird! Thou'dst never fear the net, nor lime, |
| | The pit-fall, nor the gin? |

SON	Why should I, mother?	35
	Poor birds they are not set for.
	My father is *not* dead, for all your saying.

| LADY MACDUFF | Yes, he is dead. How wilt thou do for a father? |

| SON | Nay, how will *you* do for a husband? |

| LADY MACDUFF | Why, I can buy me twenty at any market. | 40 |

| SON | Then you'll buy 'em to sell again. |

| LADY MACDUFF | Thou speakest with all thy wit – |
| | And yet, i' faith, with wit enough for thee. |

| SON | Was my father a traitor, mother? |

| LADY MACDUFF | Ay, that he was. | 45 |

| SON | What is a traitor? |

| LADY MACDUFF | Why, one that swears and lies. |

| SON | And be all traitors that do so? |

| LADY MACDUFF | Every one that does so is a traitor, and must be hanged. |

| SON | And must they all be hanged that swear and lie? | 50 |

| LADY MACDUFF | Every one. |

| SON | Who must hang them? |

| LADY MACDUFF | Why, the honest men. |

A messenger arrives and warns Lady Macduff that danger is approaching. While Lady Macduff is thinking about what to do, murderers burst in, asking for Macduff.

59 would not: i.e. didn't weep for him

62 prattler: chatterbox

64 in your … perfect: I know your rank perfectly well
65 doubt: suspect
66 homely: humble
67 Hence: Get away from here
68 savage: cruel
69 fell: terrible
70 nigh: close to
71 abide: stay
       Whither … fly: Where could I run away to

74 laudable: praiseworthy
75 Accounted: considered
       folly: foolishness / stupidity

79 unsanctified: unholy

81 shag-haired: i.e. scruffy

THINK ABOUT for GCSE

Performance and staging

• Like the old man in Act 2 Scene 4, the third murderer in Act 3 Scene 3, and the lord in Act 3 Scene 6, we don't know who the messenger is. What are the advantages of (a) keeping him anonymous; or (b) showing him to be a character we have seen earlier in the play?

Son	Then the liars and swearers are fools. For there are liars and swearers enough to beat the honest men, and hang up them.
Lady Macduff	Now God help thee, poor monkey! But how wilt thou do for a father?
Son	If he were dead, you'd weep for him. If you would not, it were a good sign that I should quickly have a new father.
Lady Macduff	Poor prattler, how thou talk'st!

Enter a Messenger.

Messenger	Bless you, fair dame! I am not to you known,
	Though in your state of honour I am perfect.
	I doubt some danger does approach you nearly.
	If you will take a homely man's advice,
	Be not found here. Hence, with your little ones.
	To fright you thus, methinks, I am too savage;
	To do worse to you were fell cruelty,
	Which is too nigh your person. Heaven preserve you!
	I dare abide no longer.

Exit.

Lady Macduff	Whither should I fly?
	I have done no harm. But I remember now
	I am in this earthly world, where to do harm
	Is often laudable, to do good sometime
	Accounted dangerous folly. Why then, alas,
	Do I put up that womanly defence,
	To say I have done no harm? –

Enter Murderers.

	What are these faces?
Murderer	Where is your husband?
Lady Macduff	I hope in no place so unsanctified,
	Where such as thou may'st find him.
Murderer	He's a traitor.
Son	Thou liest, thou shag-haired villain!

55

60

65

70

75

80

The men kill Lady Macduff's son and chase after her as she tries to escape.

81–2 egg … fry: Insulting terms for offspring or small children.

THINK ABOUT *for* GCSE

Structure and form

- Before this scene begins, we already know that Macbeth is a bloody murderer. So what effect does the scene have? How might it affect an audience's feelings?

MURDERER   What, you egg! –

Stabbing him.

            Young fry of treachery!

SON   He has killed me, mother.
            Run away, I pray you!

                                                    Dies.

Exit LADY MACDUFF, *crying out 'Murder!', with the* MURDERERS
                                            pursuing her.

In this scene ...

- In England, Macduff hopes to persuade Malcolm to return to Scotland and overthrow Macbeth.
- Having tested Macduff's loyalty, Malcolm reveals that he has an army and is prepared to invade.
- Ross arrives and tells Macduff that his family has been killed.
- Malcolm tries to comfort Macduff and they prepare to march north to do battle with Macbeth.

In England, Malcolm is visited by Macduff who wants him to lead an army back to Scotland and overthrow Macbeth. Malcolm is suspicious, fearing that Macduff might have been sent by Macbeth and might betray him to Macbeth for personal reward.

2   **bosoms**: hearts

3   **mortal**: deadly
4   **Bestride ... birthdom**: defend the fallen kingdom of our birth
6   **that it resounds**: so that it echoes

8   **Like ... dolour**: a similar mournful noise
    wail: weep for
9   **redress**: put right

10   **the ... friend**: the times are favourable
11   **perchance**: perhaps
12   **sole**: mere

14–15   **but ... me**: but you might be able to use me to get some reward from him
15   **wisdom**: i.e. you might think it wise
16   **weak ... lamb**: i.e. Macduff might offer Malcolm to Macbeth as a sacrifice
17   **appease**: calm the anger of

19–20   **may recoil ... charge**: may behave wickedly on the orders of a king
21   **transpose**: change
22   **the brightest fell**: the brightest angel, Lucifer, became a devil
23–4   **Though ... so**: Although evil people try to appear good, many others who appear virtuous genuinely are so

26   **rawness**: unprotected state
27   **motives**: people inspiring love, i.e. Macduff's wife and children

THINK ABOUT for GCSE

Structure and form

- What is the effect of the dramatic irony in what Macduff says in lines 4 to 8, and Malcolm's 'He hath not touched you yet' (line 14)?

England: the palace of King Edward.

Enter MALCOLM, *with* MACDUFF.

MALCOLM	Let us seek out some desolate shade, and there Weep our sad bosoms empty.
MACDUFF	Let us rather Hold fast the mortal sword, and like good men Bestride our down-fall birthdom. Each new morn, New widows howl, new orphans cry. New sorrows 5 Strike heaven on the face, that it resounds As if it felt with Scotland, and yelled out Like syllable of dolour.
MALCOLM	What I believe, I'll wail; What know, believe; and what I can redress – As I shall find the time to friend, I will. 10 What you have spoke, it may be so, perchance. This tyrant, whose sole name blisters our tongues, Was once thought honest: you have loved him well. He hath not touched you yet. I am young – but something You may deserve of him through me, and wisdom 15 To offer up a weak, poor, innocent lamb, To appease an angry god.
MACDUFF	I am not treacherous.
MALCOLM	But Macbeth is. A good and virtuous nature may recoil In an imperial charge. But I shall crave your pardon: 20 That which you are, my thoughts cannot transpose. Angels are bright still, though the brightest fell. Though all things foul would wear the brows of grace, Yet grace must still look so.
MACDUFF	I have lost my hopes.
MALCOLM	Perchance even there, where I did find my doubts. 25 Why in that rawness left you wife and child (Those precious motives, those strong knots of love)

Macduff is upset that Malcolm should suspect him of trying to deceive him. Still unsure whether or not Macduff can be trusted, Malcolm tests his loyalty by pretending that he himself is full of faults and vices.

29–30 Let … safeties: I am not suspicious because you have behaved dishonourably, but because I fear for my own safety

30 rightly just: genuinely honest

32 lay … sure: you can lay secure foundations

33 goodness … thee: good people are afraid to stop you
Wear … wrongs: Display your evil deeds openly

34 affeered: legally confirmed

36 space: country

37 to boot: as well

39 sinks … yoke: is dragged down by tyranny

41 withal: in addition to this

42 hands … right: people willing to fight on my side
gracious England: i.e. King Edward the Confessor

46 wear … sword: i.e. cut off Macbeth's head and spear it on the end of my sword

48 sundry: varied

49 What … be: Who are you talking about

51 All … grafted: all the individual vices are so firmly rooted in me

52 shall be opened: are revealed

54 Esteem: judge

55 confineless harms: boundless evils
legions: armies of devils

57 top: outdo in evils

THINK ABOUT *for* GCSE

Characterisation

• What is Malcolm suspicious about? Look, for example, at his comment to Macduff 'He hath not touched you yet' (line 14), as well as lines 14 to 17, and 19 to 28.

Without leave-taking? – I pray you,
Let not my jealousies be your dishonours,
But mine own safeties. You may be rightly just, 30
Whatever I shall think.

MACDUFF   Bleed, bleed, poor country!
Great tyranny, lay thou thy basis sure,
For goodness dare not check thee! Wear thou thy
    wrongs –
The title is affeered! – Fare thee well, lord.
I would not be the villain that thou think'st 35
For the whole space that's in the tyrant's grasp,
And the rich East to boot.

MALCOLM   Be not offended.
I speak not as in absolute fear of you.
I think our country sinks beneath the yoke:
It weeps, it bleeds – and each new day a gash 40
Is added to her wounds. I think, withal,
There would be hands uplifted in my right;
And here, from gracious England, have I offer
Of goodly thousands. But, for all this,
When I shall tread upon the tyrant's head, 45
Or wear it on my sword, yet my poor country
Shall have more vices than it had before,
More suffer, and more sundry ways than ever,
By him that shall succeed.

MACDUFF   What should he be?

MALCOLM   It is myself I mean – in whom I know 50
All the particulars of vice so grafted,
That, when they shall be opened, black Macbeth
Will seem as pure as snow – and the poor state
Esteem him as a lamb, being compared
With *my* confineless harms.

MACDUFF   Not in the legions 55
Of horrid hell can come a devil more damned
In evils, to top Macbeth.

Malcolm pretends that, as King, he would be even more wicked than Macbeth. He claims to be lustful and greedy. Macduff replies that Malcolm's weaknesses could be tolerated, given his good qualities.

58 **Luxurious**: lustful
avaricious: greedy
59 **Sudden**: unpredictably violent
smacking of: having a 'taste' of
61 **voluptuousness**: sexual appetite
62 **matrons**: older women
62–3 **fill ... cistern of**: i.e. satisfy
64 **All ... o'erbear**: would burst through any barriers
65 **will**: sexual desire
66 **intemperance**: lack of control
67–8 **been ... throne**: caused many a happy reign to come to an early end

71 **Convey ... plenty**: enjoy secretly
72 **seem cold**: appear to be sexually pure
the time ... hoodwink: you could deceive people in that way
75–6 **As ... inclined**: who would offer themselves to their king, if he had such desires

77 **ill-composed affection**: character made up of bad qualities
78 **staunchless avarice**: endless greed
79 **cut off**: kill
81–2 **my ... more**: the more I had, the more I would want

84–5 **This ... deeper**: This greed is a more serious weakness
85 **pernicious**: destructive
86 **summer-seeming**: i.e. which fades as you grow older
87 **sword**: i.e. reason for killing
88 **foisons**: wealth
89 **Of ... own**: even if you count just your own royal possessions
these: i.e. these vices
portable: bearable

THINK ABOUT *for* GCSE

Characterisation

- Look at the list of sins which Macbeth is guilty of, according to Malcolm (lines 57 to 59). What evidence is there for each one in the play?

142

MALCOLM   I grant him bloody,
Luxurious, avaricious, false, deceitful,
Sudden, malicious, smacking of every sin
That has a name. But there's no bottom, none,   60
In *my* voluptuousness: your wives, your daughters,
Your matrons and your maids, could not fill up
The cistern of my lust – and my desire
All continent impediments would o'erbear,
That did oppose my will. Better Macbeth   65
Than such an one to reign.

MACDUFF   Boundless intemperance
In nature is a tyranny: it hath been
Th' untimely emptying of the happy throne,
And fall of many kings. But fear not yet
To take upon you what is yours. You may   70
Convey your pleasures in a spacious plenty,
And yet seem cold – the time you may so hoodwink.
We have willing dames enough – there cannot be
That vulture in you, to devour so many
As will to greatness dedicate themselves,   75
Finding it so inclined.

MALCOLM   With this, there grows
In my most ill-composed affection such
A staunchless avarice, that, were I King,
I should cut off the nobles for their lands –
Desire his jewels, and this other's house.   80
And my more-having would be as a sauce
To make me hunger more, that I should forge
Quarrels unjust against the good and loyal,
Destroying them for wealth.

MACDUFF   This avarice
Sticks deeper, grows with more pernicious root   85
Than summer-seeming lust – and it hath been
The sword of our slain kings. Yet do not fear.
Scotland hath foisons to fill up your will,
Of your mere own. All these are portable,
With other graces weighed.   90

Malcolm continues his test of Macduff's loyalty. He claims to lack all the good characteristics a king should possess. Macduff finally believes Malcolm and angrily rejects him as a fit ruler. This is the reassurance that Malcolm wanted.

91 king-becoming graces: virtues which a king ought to have

92 verity: truthfulness
temperance: moderation

93 Bounty: generosity

94 Devotion: love of God
fortitude: strength of character

95 relish: trace

95–6 abound ... crime: have lots of variations on each individual sin

98 concord: peace and harmony

99 Uproar: throw into confusion
confound: destroy

104 untitled: with no legal right to the throne

106 issue of: heir to

107 interdiction: accusation

108 does ... breed: slanders his family

111 Died ... lived: constantly prepared herself for heaven

112–13 thou ... Scotland: 1 you report about yourself; 2 which are the same as Macbeth's

115 Child of integrity: i.e. which comes from your honest character

116 black scruples: sinister suspicions

118 trains: tricks / plots

119–20 modest ... haste: cautious good sense holds me back from believing people too hastily

121 Deal ... me: i.e. bless our relationship

123 Unspeak ... detraction: take back everything I said against myself
abjure: deny

124 taints ... myself: the sins and crimes I accused myself of

125 For ... nature: i.e. as things that are not part of my character

THINK ABOUT for GCSE

Themes and issues

• **Kingship**: Which aspects of the behaviour described by Malcolm, in lines 60 to 65, 76 to 84, and 91 to 100, would be most likely to persuade Macduff – and Shakespeare's audience – that such a man was not fit to rule?

MALCOLM	But I have none. The king-becoming graces –	
	As justice, verity, temperance, stableness,	
	Bounty, perseverance, mercy, lowliness,	
	Devotion, patience, courage, fortitude –	
	I have no relish of them; but abound	95
	In the division of each several crime,	
	Acting it many ways. Nay, had I power, I should	
	Pour the sweet milk of concord into hell,	
	Uproar the universal peace, confound	
	All unity on earth.	

| MACDUFF | O Scotland! Scotland! | 100 |

| MALCOLM | If such a one be fit to govern, speak. | |
| | I am as I have spoken. | |

MACDUFF	Fit to govern?	
	No, not to live! – O nation miserable! –	
	With an untitled tyrant, bloody-sceptered!	
	When shalt thou see thy wholesome days again,	105
	Since that the truest issue of thy throne	
	By his own interdiction stands accused,	
	And does blaspheme his breed? Thy royal father	
	Was a most sainted King. The Queen that bore thee,	
	Oft'ner upon her knees than on her feet,	110
	Died every day she lived. Fare thee well!	
	These evils thou repeat'st upon thyself	
	Hath banished me from Scotland. – O my breast,	
	Thy hope ends here!	

MALCOLM	Macduff, this noble passion,	
	Child of integrity, hath from my soul	115
	Wiped the black scruples, reconciled my thoughts	
	To thy good truth and honour. Devilish Macbeth	
	By many of these trains hath sought to win me	
	Into his power, and modest wisdom plucks me	
	From over-credulous haste. But God above	120
	Deal between thee and me! For even now	
	I put myself to thy direction, and	
	Unspeak mine own detraction – here abjure	
	The taints and blames I laid upon myself	
	For strangers to my nature. I am yet	125

Malcolm explains that he was lying to test Macduff's loyalty. A doctor enters and they discuss the power of Edward the Confessor, the English King, to cure a disease known as 'the king's evil'.

THINK ABOUT for GCSE

Characterisation

• Edward the Confessor is called 'this good king': he 'solicits heaven', he cures the sick, he has the gift of prophecy, and he is famous for his virtues (lines 141 to 159). In what ways might each of these qualities or actions be contrasted with Macbeth's?

Context

• King James himself was known to have 'touched' diseased people in hope of curing them. What does this tell us about the beliefs held by many people at that time concerning kings, illness and the supernatural?

126 **Unknown to woman**: a virgin
     never was forsworn: have never lied
127 **coveted**: been envious of
128 **my faith**: a promise I had made

133 **Whither**: to Scotland
     here-approach: arrival
135 **at a point**: fully prepared for battle
136–7 **chance … quarrel**: may our chance of success be equal to the justice of our cause

139 **reconcile**: adjust my mind to
     more anon: we'll talk more later

142 **stay his cure**: are waiting to be cured by him
     malady: disease
142–3 **convinces … art**: defeats the greatest medical skill
144 **sanctity**: holy power
145 **presently amend**: instantly recover
146 **the Evil**: scrofula, a disease that English kings were said to be able to cure by touching
148 **here-remain**: stay
149 **solicits**: gets help from
150 **strangely-visited**: with strange illnesses
152 **mere … surgery**: people that doctors have completely given up on
153 **stamp**: coin
154 **'tis spoken**: it is said
155–6 **leaves … benediction**: hands on this blessed power
156 **With … virtue**: As well as this strange talent

Unknown to woman; never was forsworn;
Scarcely have coveted what was mine own;
At no time broke my faith: would not betray
The devil to his fellow – and delight
No less in truth than life. My first false speaking   130
Was this upon myself. What I am truly
Is thine, and my poor country's, to command –
Whither, indeed, before thy here-approach,
Old Siward, with ten thousand warlike men,
Already at a point, was setting forth.   135
Now we'll together, and the chance of goodness
Be like our warranted quarrel! Why are you silent?

MACDUFF   Such welcome and unwelcome things at once,
'Tis hard to reconcile.

Enter an English DOCTOR.

MALCOLM   Well, more anon. –
(*To the* DOCTOR) Comes the King forth, I pray you?   140

DOCTOR   Ay, sir. There are a crew of wretched souls
That stay his cure. Their malady convinces
The great assay of art – but, at his touch,
Such sanctity hath heaven given his hand,
They presently amend.

MALCOLM   I thank you, doctor.   145

Exit DOCTOR.

MACDUFF   What's the disease he means?

MALCOLM   'Tis called the Evil.
A most miraculous work in this good King,
Which often, since my here-remain in England,
I have seen him do. How he solicits heaven
Himself best knows; but strangely-visited people,   150
All swoll'n and ulcerous, pitiful to the eye,
The mere despair of surgery, he cures –
Hanging a golden stamp about their necks,
Put on with holy prayers. And 'tis spoken,
To the succeeding royalty he leaves   155
The healing benediction. With this strange virtue

Ross arrives with the latest news from Scotland. He describes the country's suffering under Macbeth, but then lies, telling Macduff that his family are well.

158   sundry: various
159   speak him: declare that he is

162   betimes: quickly
163   means: conditions

164   Stands ... did: Are things still the same in Scotland

166–7   nothing ... smile: the only cheerful people are those who know nothing
168   rend: tear apart / split
169   not marked: but nobody takes any notice of them
170   modern ecstasy: common emotion
170–1   The ... who: When the funeral bell tolls, people hardly bother to ask who it is for
172   Expire: come to an end
173   or ... sicken: before they have time to fall ill and die naturally
173–4   relation ... nice: this report has too many ugly details
175   That ... speaker: Anyone telling hour-old news will be booed by their audience
176   teems ... one: gives rise to fresh suffering

179   well at peace: can mean 'dead'

THINK ABOUT for GCSE

Characterisation

• Why do you think that Ross initially reports that Macduff's wife and children are well (lines 176 to 179)?

Themes and issues

• Which words and phrases in his replies can have more than one meaning? Is this an example of **equivocation** for good ends?

• **Order and nature**: What picture of Scotland under Macbeth is presented by Macduff and Malcolm in this scene?

He hath a heavenly gift of prophecy;
And sundry blessings hang about his throne
That speak him full of grace.

Enter Ross.

MACDUFF	See, who comes here?	
MALCOLM	My countryman – but yet I know him not.	**160**
MACDUFF	My ever-gentle cousin, welcome hither!	
MALCOLM	I know him now. Good God betimes remove	
	The means that makes us strangers!	
ROSS	Sir, amen.	
MACDUFF	Stands Scotland where it did?	
ROSS	Alas, poor country! –	
	Almost afraid to know itself. It cannot	**165**
	Be called our mother, but our grave – where nothing,	
	But who knows nothing, is once seen to smile;	
	Where sighs, and groans, and shrieks that rend the air	
	Are made, not marked; where violent sorrow seems	
	A modern ecstasy. The dead man's knell	**170**
	Is there scarce asked for who – and good men's lives	
	Expire before the flowers in their caps,	
	Dying or ere they sicken.	
MACDUFF	O relation	
	Too nice and yet too true!	
MALCOLM	What's the newest grief?	
ROSS	That of an hour's age doth hiss the speaker:	**175**
	Each minute teems a new one.	
MACDUFF	How does my wife?	
ROSS	Why, well.	
MACDUFF	And all my children?	
ROSS	Well, too.	
MACDUFF	The tyrant has not battered at their peace?	
ROSS	No. They were well at peace when I did leave 'em.	

Ross reports that many good men are preparing to rebel against Macbeth. Malcolm confirms his plan to invade Scotland with the support of an English army. Ross now reveals to Macduff that his family have been murdered.

THINK ABOUT for GCSE

Performance and staging

- If you were the director, how would you ask the actor playing Ross to act in lines 180 to 213? Think about how he should deliver the reports about Scotland to encourage Malcolm, and then break the news to Macduff of his family's killing.

180 **Be not ... speech**: Don't hold back

183 **out**: i.e. preparing for battle
184–5 **was ... that**: I was more prepared to believe because
185 **power afoot**: army on the march
186 **eye**: appearance

188 **doff ... distresses**: throw off their terrible miseries

191–2 **none ... out**: the Christian world cannot boast of

192 **Would**: I wish

195 **latch**: catch

196 **The general cause**: Is this bad news for everybody
196–7 **fee-grief ... breast**: personal sorrow

199 **Pertains**: belongs

202 **possess**: inform

204 **is surprised**: has been taken by surprise

206 **Were**: would be
on the ... deer: i.e. onto the pile of Macduff's slaughtered family

MACDUFF	Be not a niggard of your speech: how goes 't?	**180**

ROSS   When I came hither to transport the tidings
          Which I have heavily borne, there ran a rumour
          Of many worthy fellows that were out –
          Which was, to my belief, witnessed the rather
          For that I saw the tyrant's power afoot.   **185**
          Now is the time of help. (*To* MALCOLM) Your eye in
            Scotland
          Would create soldiers, make our women fight
          To doff their dire distresses.

MALCOLM   Be 't their comfort,
          We are coming thither. Gracious England hath
          Lent us good Siward, and ten thousand men –   **190**
          An older and a better soldier none
          That Christendom gives out.

ROSS   Would I could answer
          This comfort with the like! But I have words
          That would be howled out in the desert air,
          Where hearing should not latch them.

MACDUFF   What concern they? **195**
          The general cause? Or is it a fee-grief
          Due to some single breast?

ROSS   No mind that's honest
          But in it shares some woe, though the main part
          Pertains to you alone.

MACDUFF   If it be mine,
          Keep it not from me: quickly let me have it.   **200**

ROSS   Let not your ears despise my tongue for ever,
          Which shall possess them with the heaviest sound
          That ever yet they heard.

MACDUFF   H'm! – I guess at it.

ROSS   Your castle is surprised – your wife and babes
          Savagely slaughtered. To relate the manner   **205**
          Were, on the quarry of these murdered deer,
          To add the death of you.

Malcolm tries to comfort Macduff over the loss of his family.

208 **Ne'er ... hat**: a sign of grief

210 **o'er-fraught**: overloaded

212 **must ... thence**: had to be away from home

217 **hell-kite**: like a bird of prey from hell
218 **dam**: mother
219 **fell**: deadly

Dispute: Fight

223 **take their part**: fight on their side
224 **Naught that**: Worthless as
225 **demerits**: faults

227 **whetstone**: tool used for sharpening knives and swords
228 **Blunt ... heart**: i.e. Don't let grief deaden your spirits
229 **play the**: behave like a
230 **braggart**: boaster
231 **Cut ... intermission**: let there be no interval
Front to front: Face to face
234 **This ... manly**: i.e. That's a man's reaction
235 **power**: army
236 **Our ... leave**: All that remains for us to do is leave
237 **ripe for shaking**: i.e. like ripe fruit ready to be shaken from the tree
above: in heaven
238 **Put ... instruments**: are arming themselves
cheer: comfort
239 **The ... day**: it's a long night that has no dawn

THINK ABOUT for GCSE

Performance and staging

• Who is Macduff referring to when he says 'He has no children' (line 216) – Malcolm or Macbeth? How could you make the meaning clear in performance?

Themes and issues

• In what ways is the debate about **manhood**, and what it means to be 'a man', developed here? Look at Malcolm's statements and Macduff's replies.

MALCOLM	Merciful heaven! –
	What, man! Ne'er pull your hat upon your brows:
	Give sorrow words. The grief that does not speak
	Whispers the o'er-fraught heart, and bids it break.

210

MACDUFF	My children too?
ROSS	Wife, children, servants – all
	That could be found.
MACDUFF	And I must be from thence!
	My wife killed too?
ROSS	I have said.
MALCOLM	Be comforted.
	Let's make us medicines of our great revenge,
	To cure this deadly grief.

215

MACDUFF	He has no children. – All my pretty ones?
	Did you say all? – O hell-kite! – All?
	What, all my pretty chickens, and their dam,
	At one fell swoop?
MALCOLM	Dispute it like a man.
MACDUFF	I shall do so.
	But I must also feel it as a man:

220

	I cannot but remember such things were,
	That were most precious to me. – Did heaven look on,
	And would not take their part? Sinful Macduff!
	They were all struck for thee. Naught that I am,
	Not for their own demerits, but for mine

225

	Fell slaughter on their souls. Heaven rest them now!
MALCOLM	Be this the whetstone of your sword: let grief
	Convert to anger. Blunt not the heart, enrage it.
MACDUFF	O! I could play the woman with mine eyes,
	And braggart with my tongue. – But, gentle heavens,

230

	Cut short all intermission. Front to front
	Bring thou this fiend of Scotland and myself.
	Within my sword's length set him. If he 'scape,
	Heaven forgive him too!

Malcolm goes off with Macduff and Ross to prepare for the attack on Macbeth.

234 **This ... manly**: i.e. That's a man's reaction

235 **power**: army

236 **Our ... leave**: All that remains for us to do is leave

237 **ripe for shaking**: i.e. like ripe fruit ready to be shaken from the tree
above: in heaven

238 **Put ... instruments**: are arming themselves
cheer: comfort

239 **The ... day**: it's a long night that has no dawn

THINK ABOUT for GCSE

Characterisation

- What impression have you received of Malcolm from this scene? Look, for example, at the way he deals with Macduff, and at his final speech (lines 234 to 239). What kind of king is he likely to be?

Performance and staging

- If you were the director, would you stage this scene in light, pleasant surroundings or in gloom? What effect could each setting have?

MALCOLM   This tune goes manly.
Come, go we to the King. Our power is ready –   **235**
Our lack is nothing but our leave. Macbeth
Is ripe for shaking, and the powers above
Put on their instruments. Receive what cheer you may:
The night is long that never finds the day.

                                                    Exeunt.

In this scene ...

- Lady Macbeth's doctor and gentlewoman watch her sleepwalking.
- They see that her mind is tormented by guilt and horror at the murders that have been committed.

Lady Macbeth's gentlewoman tells a doctor about her strange behaviour. She appears, walking in her sleep.

THINK ABOUT for GCSE

Performance and staging

- If you were the director, what advice would you give to the actress playing Lady Macbeth about this scene? Think about her movements and actions, how she should speak the lines, where she should pause, her facial expressions, and what emotions the character is experiencing.

Characterisation

- What do you think Lady Macbeth writes on the paper mentioned by her gentlewoman (lines 3 to 7)?

Themes and issues

- What does this scene contribute to the theme of **kingship**?

1   **watched**: kept watch

3   **went ... field**: led his army (against the rebels)
5   **closet**: private chest for valuables

8   **perturbation in nature**: disorder in her mind and body
    at once: at the same time
9   **do ... watching**: behave as though awake
10 **slumbery agitation**: physical activity while asleep
11 **actual performances**: things you have actually seen her do
13 **after her**: that she said
14 **most meet**: appropriate

17 **Lo you**: Look
    her very guise: the way she behaved before
18 **stand close**: keep out of sight

23 **their ... shut**: i.e. she is not actually seeing anything

25 **accustomed**: usual / frequent

Inside Macbeth's castle at Dunsinane.

Enter a DOCTOR, *with a* WAITING-GENTLEWOMAN.

DOCTOR	I have two nights watched with you, but can perceive no truth in your report. When was it she last walked?
GENTLEWOMAN	Since his Majesty went into the field, I have seen her rise from her bed, throw her night-gown upon her, unlock her closet, take forth paper, fold it, write upon 't, **5** read it, afterwards seal it, and again return to bed – yet all this while in a most fast sleep.
DOCTOR	A great perturbation in nature, to receive at once the benefit of sleep, and do the effects of watching! In this slumbery agitation, besides her walking and other **10** actual performances, what, at any time, have you heard her say?
GENTLEWOMAN	That, sir, which I will not report after her.
DOCTOR	You may to me; and 'tis most meet you should.
GENTLEWOMAN	Neither to you, nor any one, having no witness to **15** confirm my speech.

Enter LADY MACBETH *in her night-gown, with a candle.*

	Lo you! Here she comes. This is her very guise – and, upon my life, fast asleep. Observe her: stand close.
DOCTOR	How came she by that light?
GENTLEWOMAN	Why, it stood by her. She has light by her continually – **20** 'tis her command.
DOCTOR	You see, her eyes are open.
GENTLEWOMAN	Ay, but their sense are shut.
DOCTOR	What is it she does now? Look, how she rubs her hands.
GENTLEWOMAN	It is an accustomed action with her, to seem thus **25** washing her hands. I have known her continue in this a quarter of an hour.

In her sleepwalking Lady Macbeth imagines that she is washing blood off her hands. It seems that she is talking to her husband in her sleep about the murders that he and his followers have committed.

29 **set**: write
30 **satisfy my remembrance**: back up my memory
31 **One, two**: She imagines she hears a bell (see Act 2 Scene 1, line 63).
32 **Fie**: Shame on you
33 **afeard**: afraid
34 **none ... account**: we are so powerful that nobody can challenge what we have done
37 **mark**: hear
38 **Thane of Fife**: i.e. Macduff

40 **mar all**: ruin everything
41 **starting**: nervousness / jumpiness

42 **Go to**: i.e. That's bad

47 **sorely charged**: carrying a heavy burden (of guilt)
49 **dignity**: worth / value

THINK ABOUT for GCSE

Performance and staging

• In a film version, it would be possible to show what is going on in Lady Macbeth's head. How could this be done and what images might be shown?

52 **practice**: skill as a doctor
53–4 **died holily**: i.e. with clear consciences

57 **on's**: of his
58 **Even so**: So is that the way things are

LADY MACBETH   Yet here's a spot.

DOCTOR   Hark! She speaks. I will set down what comes from her, to satisfy my remembrance the more strongly.   30

LADY MACBETH   Out, damned spot! Out, I say! – One, two. Why, then 'tis time to do it. – Hell is murky. – Fie, my lord, fie! – a soldier, and afeard? – What need we fear who knows it, when none can call our power to account? – Yet who would have thought the old man to have had so much   35 blood in him?

DOCTOR   Do you mark that?

LADY MACBETH   The Thane of Fife had a wife: where is she now? – What, will these hands ne'er be clean? – No more o' that, my lord, no more o' that: you mar all with this   40 starting.

DOCTOR   Go to, go to: you have known what you should not.

GENTLEWOMAN   She has spoke what she should not, I am sure of that. Heaven knows what she has known.

LADY MACBETH   Here's the smell of the blood still! All the perfumes of   45 Arabia will not sweeten this little hand. O! Oh, oh –

DOCTOR   What a sigh is there! The heart is sorely charged.

GENTLEWOMAN   I would not have such a heart in my bosom for the dignity of the whole body.

DOCTOR   Well, well, well –   50

GENTLEWOMAN   Pray God it be, sir.

DOCTOR   This disease is beyond my practice. Yet I have known those which have walked in their sleep, who have died holily in their beds.

LADY MACBETH   Wash your hands, put on your night-gown. Look   55 not so pale. – I tell you yet again, Banquo's buried: he cannot come out on's grave.

DOCTOR   Even so?

Lady Macbeth goes back to bed and the Doctor leaves, shocked by what he has seen and heard.

63 **Directly**: Immediately

64 **Foul ... abroad**: Terrible rumours are going around

65 **infected**: diseased

66 **discharge**: reveal

67 **More ... physician**: She needs a priest more than a doctor

69 **means ... annoyance**: anything that she might harm herself with

70 **still**: always

71 **mated**: bewildered

THINK ABOUT for GCSE

Themes and issues

* Minor characters in Shakespeare's plays are often extremely important. What does the Doctor say in his final speech (lines 64 to 72) which adds to our understanding of Scotland under Macbeth's rule? How do his words contribute to the theme of **order and nature**?

Structure and form

* What events earlier in the play do Lady Macbeth's speeches and actions in this scene refer to?

LADY MACBETH	To bed, to bed: there's knocking at the gate! Come, come, come, come, give me your hand. What's done **60** cannot be undone. To bed, to bed, to bed.

Exit.

DOCTOR	Will she go now to bed?
GENTLEWOMAN	Directly.
DOCTOR	Foul whisp'rings are abroad. Unnatural deeds Do breed unnatural troubles: infected minds **65** To their deaf pillows will discharge their secrets. More needs she the divine than the physician. – God, God forgive us all! Look after her. Remove from her the means of all annoyance, And still keep eyes upon her. – So, goodnight. **70** My mind she has mated, and amazed my sight. I think, but dare not speak.
GENTLEWOMAN	Goodnight, good doctor.

Exeunt.

In this scene ...

- The army of Scottish lords formed to overthrow Macbeth approaches Macbeth's castle at Dunsinane, ready to meet up with Malcolm.
- The lords discuss Macbeth's loss of control.

The army of Scottish lords marches to join up with Malcolm, Macduff and the English forces. They discuss reports that Macbeth has taken refuge in his castle, and that people are now following him out of fear, not loyalty.

THINK ABOUT for GCSE

Language

- What does the clothing imagery in lines 15 to 22 tell us about the Thanes' opinions of (a) Macbeth's control of his kingdom; and (b) his fitness to bear the great title of King?

Themes and issues

- How do these images contribute to the theme of **kingship**?

1 **power**: army

3 **their dear causes**: the terrible wrongs done against them

4–5 **to the ... man**: be enough to make a dead or paralysed man want to join in the bloodshed and din of battle

6 **well**: probably

8 **file**: list

9 **gentry**: noblemen

10 **unrough**: unbearded, i.e. young

11 **Protest ... manhood**: show that they are now acting like men for the first time

14 **valiant fury**: mad courage

15 **distempered**: swollen with disease

18 **Now ... faith-breach**: Every minute rebellions attack him for his disloyalty

19–20 **move ... love**: only obey him because they are following orders, not because they love him

23 **pestered senses**: troubled nerves
     to recoil and start: i.e. for being jumpy

24–5 **all ... there**: i.e. his whole inner being is sickened at the thought of what he has become

ACT 5   SCENE 2

Open country near Dunsinane.

Enter soldiers, with drums beating and banners.

Enter MENTEITH, CAITHNESS, ANGUS, *and* LENNOX.

MENTEITH	The English power is near, led on by Malcolm,
	His uncle Siward, and the good Macduff.
	Revenges burn in them – for their dear causes
	Would to the bleeding and the grim alarm
	Excite the mortified man.

ANGUS   Near Birnam wood   5
Shall we well meet them: that way are they coming.

CAITHNESS   Who knows if Donalbain be with his brother?

LENNOX   For certain, sir, he is not. I have a file
Of all the gentry. There is Siward's son,
And many unrough youths, that even now   10
Protest their first of manhood.

MENTEITH   What does the tyrant?

CAITHNESS   Great Dunsinane he strongly fortifies.
Some say he's mad. Others, that lesser hate him,
Do call it valiant fury – but for certain,
He cannot buckle his distempered cause   15
Within the belt of rule.

ANGUS   Now does he feel
His secret murders sticking on his hands.
Now minutely revolts upbraid his faith-breach:
Those he commands move only in command,
Nothing in love. Now does he feel his title   20
Hang loose about him, like a giant's robe
Upon a dwarfish thief.

MENTEITH   Who then shall blame
His pestered senses to recoil and start,
When all that is within him does condemn
Itself for being there?

The army of Scottish lords
marches on towards Birnam.

27 **Meet ... weal**: Let's meet the doctor to
    this diseased country (i.e. Malcolm)
28 **purge**: cleansing medicine

30 **dew**: water
    sovereign: 1 royal; 2 with power as
    medicine

THINK ABOUT *for* GCSE

Language

• What two different images
  do Caithness and Lennox
  use in their final speeches
  (lines 25 to 31)? How
  effective is each image in
  suggesting the parts that
  Malcolm and the lords will
  have to play in making
  Scotland a good country to
  live in?

• How do these images link
  with others about Scotland
  in Act 4?

Themes and issues

• In what ways do the images
  contribute to the theme of
  order and nature?

CAITHNESS	Well, march we on, 25
	To give obedience where 'tis truly owed.
	Meet we the medicine of the sickly weal –
	And with him pour we, in our country's purge,
	Each drop of us.
LENNOX	Or so much as it needs
	To dew the sovereign flower and drown the weeds. 30
	Make we our march towards Birnam.

Drums beat again. Exeunt, marching.

In this scene ...

- In his castle, Macbeth refuses to hear any more reports of the forces facing him, confident that he cannot be harmed.
- The Doctor reports that Lady Macbeth is sick in her mind.
- Macbeth prepares to fight, armed with the Witches' predictions.

Macbeth receives reports of the approaching armies, but takes comfort in the Witches' predictions.

THINK ABOUT for GCSE

Characterisation

- What does Macbeth's treatment of his servants reveal about his state of mind?

Structure and form

- Check that you recall the wording of the prophecies which are giving Macbeth confidence here (lines 2 to 7). What effect have those prophecies had on Macbeth's mood here, and his attitude towards the attacking forces?

1 **Let ... all**: I don't care if they all desert me
3 **taint**: become weak with

5 **All ... consequences**: everything that will happen to human beings
7 **false**: treacherous

8 **epicures**: people who live soft lives
9 **sway**: rule myself

11 **cream-faced loon**: idiot, white with fear
12 **goose look**: look of a foolish goose

14 **prick ... fear**: smear your face with blood to cover the paleness
15 **lily-livered**: cowardly
   patch: clown / fool
16 **linen**: i.e. bleached white
17 **are ... fear**: persuade others to be afraid
   whey-face: white with fear
20 **push**: attack
21 **disseat me**: throw me off my throne

23 **Is ... sere**: has become withered (like a dying plant)
25 **As**: such as

Dunsinane: inside the castle.

Enter MACBETH, *with the* DOCTOR *and attendants.*

MACBETH   Bring me no more reports! Let them fly all!
Till Birnam wood remove to Dunsinane
I cannot taint with fear. What's the boy Malcolm?
Was he not born of woman? The spirits that know
All mortal consequences have pronounced me thus: 5
'Fear not, Macbeth: no man that's born of woman
Shall e'er have power upon thee.' – Then fly, false
        thanes,
And mingle with the English epicures.
The mind I sway by, and the heart I bear,
Shall never sag with doubt, nor shake with fear.   10

Enter a SERVANT.

The devil damn thee black, thou cream-faced loon!
Where got'st thou that goose look?

SERVANT   There is ten thousand –

MACBETH   Geese, villain?

SERVANT   Soldiers, sir.

MACBETH   Go, prick thy face and over-red thy fear,
Thou lily-livered boy. What soldiers, patch?   15
Death of thy soul! Those linen cheeks of thine
Are counsellors to fear. What soldiers, whey-face?

SERVANT   The English force, so please you.

MACBETH   Take thy face hence! – (*Exit* SERVANT) – Seyton! – I am
        sick at heart,
When I behold – Seyton, I say! – This push   20
Will cheer me ever, or disseat me now.
I have lived long enough. My way of life
Is fall'n into the sere, the yellow leaf –
And that which should accompany old age,
As honour, love, obedience, troops of friends,   25

Macbeth faces the fact that he cannot look forward to an old age of happiness and respect. The Doctor reports that Lady Macbeth is sick in her mind.

26 must ... have: cannot expect
stead: place
27 mouth-honour: flattery
27–8 breath ... deny: words which are mere air and which the speaker would prefer to deny having said

35 skirr: scour / raid through

38 As ... fancies: rather that she is disturbed by persistent hallucinations
40 minister to: treat (as a doctor)
42 Raze out: erase / rub out
43 oblivious antidote: medicine which would help her forget
44 stuffed bosom: over-full heart
perilous stuff: dangerous, tormenting thoughts
45–6 Therein ... himself: That is something that the patient has to provide their own treatment for
47 physic: medicine
48 staff: a mace, carried to show that he is King
50 dispatch: get on with it
50–1 cast ... land: analyse the urine (to find what disease the patient has)
52 purge ... health: cleanse it to its original good health

THINK ABOUT
for **GCSE**

Characterisation

• What exactly does Macbeth seem to be regretting in lines 22 to 28? Do you feel any sympathy for him here?

I must not look to have – but in their stead,
Curses, not loud but deep, mouth-honour, breath,
Which the poor heart would fain deny, and dare not.
Seyton!

Enter SEYTON.

SEYTON	What's your gracious pleasure?	
MACBETH	What news more?	30
SEYTON	All is confirmed, my lord, which was reported.	
MACBETH	I'll fight, till from my bones my flesh be hacked! Give me my armour.	
SEYTON	'Tis not needed yet.	
MACBETH	I'll put it on. Send out more horses, skirr the country round. Hang those that talk of fear. Give me mine armour. – How does your patient, doctor?	35
DOCTOR	Not so sick, my lord, As she is troubled with thick-coming fancies, That keep her from her rest.	
MACBETH	Cure her of that. – Canst thou not minister to a mind diseased, Pluck from the memory a rooted sorrow, Raze out the written troubles of the brain, And with some sweet, oblivious antidote Cleanse the stuffed bosom of that perilous stuff Which weighs upon the heart?	40
DOCTOR	Therein the patient Must minister to himself.	45

MACBETH	Throw physic to the dogs! I'll none of it. –
	(*To* SEYTON) Come, put mine armour on. Give me my
	    staff.
	Seyton, send out. – Doctor, the thanes fly from me. –
	(*To* SEYTON) Come, sir, dispatch! – If thou couldst,
	    doctor, cast
	The water of my land, find her disease,
	And purge it to a sound and pristine health,
		50

As Macbeth puts on his armour, the Doctor leaves, wishing he were far away from Dunsinane.

55 **rhubarb ... drug**: laxatives

THINK ABOUT for GCSE

59 **bane**: destruction

Performance and staging

- Macbeth punctuates his conversation with the Doctor with a series of orders to Seyton (lines 33 to 36, 48, 50, 54 and 58). Create a list of instructions for the actors, advising them what to do at each step.

62 **Profit**: financial reward

Structure and form

- What do Macbeth's instructions to Seyton add here? How would the scene be different if it simply showed an uninterrupted exchange between Macbeth and the Doctor?

Language

- In what ways is Macbeth continuing the imagery of medicine used by the lords at the end of Act 5 Scene 2? What is he saying through the imagery in lines 55 to 56?

I would applaud thee to the very echo,
That should applaud again. – (*To* SEYTON) Pull 't off, I
  say! –
(*To the* DOCTOR) What rhubarb, senna, or what
  purgative drug,   55
Would scour these English hence? – Hear'st thou of
  them?

DOCTOR   Ay, my good lord: your royal preparation
Makes us hear something.

MACBETH   (*To* SEYTON) Bring it after me. –
I will not be afraid of death and bane
Till Birnam forest come to Dunsinane.   60

Exit, followed by SEYTON *and attendants.*

DOCTOR   Were I from Dunsinane away and clear,
Profit again should hardly draw me here.

Exit.

In this scene ...

- Malcolm orders every man to cut down and carry a bough from Birnam Wood so that it will be hard to see how big his army is.
- He reports that many men have deserted Macbeth.

2 **chambers**: bedrooms

We ... nothing: We have no doubt of it

4 **hew**: cut
5 **shadow**: conceal
6 **numbers ... host**: size of our army
discovery: people who spy on us
7 **Err ... us**: give mistaken reports about us
8 **We ... but**: All we know is that
9–10 **will ... before 't**: is willing to let us lay siege to it
11 **where ... gone**: whenever they see an opportunity to get away
12 **more and less**: i.e. nobles and common soldiers
13 **constrainèd things**: wretched men forced to fight
14–15 **Let ... event**: i.e. We will only know after the battle whether the reports are true or not
15–16 **put ... soldiership**: behave like efficient soldiers
17 **due decision**: correct assessment
18 **shall say we have**: can claim to have achieved
owe: possess
19 **Thoughts ... relate**: Guesswork builds up our hopes
20 **certain ... arbitrate**: it is the fighting that decides the actual outcome

THINK ABOUT *for* **GCSE**

Structure and form

- As soon as Menteith informs Malcolm that this is 'The wood of Birnam' (line 3), what should we recall and what predictions might we make?

Performance and staging

- If you were the director, how would you stage in the theatre the moment when the soldiers are ordered to cut down boughs from the trees (lines 4 to 7)?

Near Dunsinane: the edge of Birnam forest.

Enter soldiers, with drums beating and banners.

Enter MALCOLM, SIWARD *and his son* (YOUNG SIWARD), MACDUFF, MENTEITH, CAITHNESS, ANGUS, LENNOX, *and* ROSS.

MALCOLM	Cousins, I hope the days are near at hand That chambers will be safe.	
MENTEITH	We doubt it nothing.	
SIWARD	What wood is this before us?	
MENTEITH	The wood of Birnam.	
MALCOLM	Let every soldier hew him down a bough, And bear 't before him. Thereby shall we shadow The numbers of our host, and make discovery Err in report of us.	5
A SOLDIER	It shall be done.	
SIWARD	We learn no other but the confident tyrant Keeps still in Dunsinane, and will endure Our setting down before 't.	
MALCOLM	'Tis his main hope. For where there is advantage to be gone, Both more and less have given him the revolt, And none serve with him but constrainèd things, Whose hearts are absent too.	10
MACDUFF	Let our just censures Attend the true event, and put we on Industrious soldiership.	15
SIWARD	The time approaches That will, with due decision, make us know What we shall say we have, and what we owe. Thoughts speculative their unsure hopes relate, But certain issue strokes must arbitrate – Towards which, advance the war!	20

Drums beat again. Exeunt, marching.

In this scene ...

- Macbeth is told that Lady Macbeth is dead.
- When Birnam Wood begins to move, his earlier confidence in the Witches' prophecies is shaken.
- Macbeth resolves to die fighting.

Boasting that his castle can stand a siege of any length, Macbeth is disturbed by a sudden cry of women. Receiving the news that Lady Macbeth is dead, he thinks about life and death.

THINK ABOUT for GCSE

Language

- Among other possibilities, line 18 could mean (a) there was a time when I could have responded to such news; (b) the word would have to be spoken at some time; or (c) there would have been a better time for such news. Which of these meanings best fits your interpretation of the play so far?

Relationships

- Considering Act 5 Scene 3 and this scene, how do you think Macbeth has come to feel about his wife?

4 **famine**: starvation
ague: fever
5 **forced ... ours**: reinforced with people who should be on our side
6 **dareful ... beard**: defiantly in open battle

11 **fell of hair**: hair on my skin
12 **dismal treatise**: frightening story
13 **supped full with**: had my fill of
14 **Direness**: horror
slaughterous thoughts: murderous mind
15 **once start me**: shock me now
Wherefore ... cry: What was that cry about
17 **She ... hereafter**: 1 she ought to have died some time in the future; 2 she would have had to die some time or other
19–21 **Tomorrow ... time**: Each day follows the next, creeping along, until the last word has been written down in the book of time
22–3 **lighted ... death**: provided a light for fools on their journey to the grave
24 **poor player**: 1 unfortunate; 2 incompetent actor
25 **struts and frets**: swaggers and talks agitatedly

Dunsinane: inside the castle.

Drums beat a call to arms. Enter MACBETH, SEYTON, *and soldiers with Macbeth's banner.*

MACBETH	Hang out our banners on the outward walls.
	The cry is still, 'They come!' Our castle's strength
	Will laugh a siege to scorn. Here let them lie,
	Till famine and the ague eat them up!
	Were they not forced with those that should be ours, 5
	We might have met them dareful, beard to beard,
	And beat them backward home. (*A sudden sound of*
	women's cries is heard.) What is that noise?
SEYTON	It is the cry of women, my good lord.

Exit.

MACBETH	I have almost forgot the taste of fears.
	The time has been, my senses would have cooled 10
	To hear a night-shriek; and my fell of hair
	Would, at a dismal treatise, rouse and stir,
	As life were in 't. I have supped full with horrors:
	Direness, familiar to my slaughterous thoughts,
	Cannot once start me.

Re-enter SEYTON.

Wherefore was that cry? 15

SEYTON	The Queen, my lord, is dead.
MACBETH	She should have died hereafter:
	There would have been a time for such a word. –
	Tomorrow, and tomorrow, and tomorrow,
	Creeps in this petty pace from day to day, 20
	To the last syllable of recorded time –
	And all our yesterdays have lighted fools
	The way to dusty death. Out, out, brief candle!
	Life's but a walking shadow, a poor player
	That struts and frets his hour upon the stage, 25

When a messenger reports that Birnam Wood appears to be moving, Macbeth begins to realise that the Witches have deceived him. Now feeling tired of life, he decides to fight to the end.

THINK ABOUT *for* **GCSE**

Characterisation

- What is Macbeth's view of life conveyed in his soliloquy (speech in which he shares his private thoughts with the audience) in lines 19 to 28?

Language

- How are the soliloquy's ideas conveyed through images of the theatre?

Themes and issues

- Macbeth begins to doubt 'th' equivocation of the fiend, | That lies like truth' (lines 43 to 44). How effective is that phrase in helping us to understand the nature of **equivocation** in this play?

---

31 **should**: 1 ought to; 2 want to

34 **anon**: suddenly

36 **endure your wrath**: suffer your anger

38 **grove**: wood

39 **next**: nearest

40 **Till ... thee**: until you shrivel up from starvation
   sooth: truth

42 **pull in resolution**: am beginning to lose my determination

43 **doubt ... fiend**: be suspicious of the devil who tells me one thing and means something else

44 **That ... truth**: which make lies sound like truth

47 **avouches**: claims

48 **nor ... tarrying**: no escape by running away or by staying here

49 **'gin ... sun**: am beginning to be tired of life

50 **th' estate ... undone**: that the universe would fall apart

51 **wrack**: destruction

52 **harness**: armour

And then is heard no more. It is a tale
Told by an idiot, full of sound and fury,
Signifying nothing.

Enter a MESSENGER.

Thou com'st to use thy tongue: thy story, quickly.

MESSENGER	Gracious my lord,	30

I should report that which I say I saw,
But know not how to do it.

MACBETH   Well: say, sir.

MESSENGER As I did stand my watch upon the hill,
I looked toward Birnam, and anon, methought,
The wood began to move.

MACBETH   Liar and slave!   35

MESSENGER Let me endure your wrath, if 't be not so.
Within this three mile may you see it coming. –
I say, a moving grove.

MACBETH   If thou speak'st false,
Upon the next tree shalt thou hang alive,
Till famine cling thee! If thy speech be sooth,   40
I care not if thou dost for me as much. –
I pull in resolution, and begin
To doubt th' equivocation of the fiend,
That lies like truth. 'Fear not, till Birnam wood
Do come to Dunsinane' – and now a wood   45
Comes toward Dunsinane. – Arm! Arm, and out! –
If this which he avouches does appear,
There is nor flying hence, nor tarrying here.
I 'gin to be aweary of the sun,
And wish th' estate o' th' world were now undone.   50
Ring the alarum bell! – Blow, wind! Come, wrack!
At least we'll die with harness on our back.

Exeunt.

In this scene ...

- Malcolm instructs Siward and his son to take charge of the leading regiments.
- Malcolm then orders the trumpets to sound.

2   **show ... are**: let the enemy see you as you really are

4   **first battle**: the main part of the army

6   **order**: battle plan

7   **Do we but**: If we can only

10   **clamorous harbingers**: noisy announcers

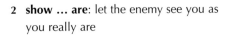

THINK ABOUT for GCSE

Performance and staging

- Think about the staging of Act 5 Scenes 5, 6 and 7. What purposes does the short Scene 6 have?

Dunsinane: open ground outside the castle.

Enter soldiers, with drum and banners. Others carry green branches from the forest. Enter Malcolm *and* Siward, *with* Macduff.

Malcolm	Now, near enough: your leafy screens throw down,
	And show like those you are. – (*To* Siward) You,
	worthy uncle,
	Shall with my cousin, your right noble son,
	Lead our first battle. Worthy Macduff and we
	Shall take upon 's what else remains to do, 5
	According to our order.
Siward	Fare you well. –
	Do we but find the tyrant's power tonight,
	Let us be beaten, if we cannot fight.
Macduff	Make all our trumpets speak! – Give them all breath –
	Those clamorous harbingers of blood and death. 10

Drums beat a call to arms, and trumpets sound. Exeunt.

In this scene ...

- Battle has begun. Macbeth kills Young Siward, but his castle is soon surrendered.
- Macduff searches the battlefield for Macbeth.

Macbeth kills Siward's son, confident that he cannot be harmed by any man born of woman. Macduff is hunting for Macbeth, determined that he should be the one to kill him.

THINK ABOUT for GCSE

Characterisation

- What are Macbeth's feelings and attitudes as the battle begins? Look at Act 5 Scene 5, lines 42 to 44, 49 to 50, and 51 to 52, and Act 5 Scene 7, lines 1 to 4.

- How might Macbeth be affected by the realisation that the Witches equivocated in one of their key predictions?

2 **bear-like ... course**: i.e. I have no choice but to fight it out (a reference to bear-baiting with dogs)
What's he: What man exists

10 **abhorrèd**: detested

15 **with ... mine**: i.e. if anybody else has killed you
17 **kerns**: Irish foot-soldiers
18 **hired**: i.e. they are paid to fight
staves: spears
Either thou: I will either fight you
19 **unbattered**: undamaged (because he would not have used it)

Battlefield, near the castle gates.

Trumpet calls and noise of fighting.

Enter MACBETH.

MACBETH	They have tied me to a stake: I cannot fly,
	But, bear-like, I must fight the course. – What's he
	That was not born of woman? Such a one
	Am I to fear, or none.

Enter YOUNG SIWARD.

YOUNG SIWARD What is thy name?

MACBETH   Thou'lt be afraid to hear it.   5

YOUNG SIWARD No! – though thou call'st thyself a hotter name
Than any is in hell.

MACBETH   My name's Macbeth.

YOUNG SIWARD The devil himself could not pronounce a title
More hateful to mine ear.

MACBETH   No, nor more fearful.

YOUNG SIWARD Thou liest, abhorrèd tyrant! With my sword   10
I'll prove the lie thou speak'st.

They fight. YOUNG SIWARD *is killed.*

MACBETH   Thou wast born of woman.
– But swords I smile at, weapons laugh to scorn,
Brandished by man that's of a woman born.

Exit.

Noise of battle continues. Enter MACDUFF.

MACDUFF   That way the noise is. – Tyrant, show thy face! –
If thou be'st slain, and with no stroke of mine,   15
My wife and children's ghosts will haunt me still.
I cannot strike at wretched kerns, whose arms
Are hired to bear their staves. Either thou, Macbeth! –
Or else my sword, with an unbattered edge,

With Macbeth's forces almost defeated, Malcolm and Old Siward victoriously enter the castle.

20 **sheathe**: replace in its sheath
   undeeded: unused

21–2 **By this ... bruited**: i.e. There is so much noise that someone important must be here

23 **And ... not**: That's all I ask

24 **gently rendered**: surrendered without much fighting

27 **The day ... yours**: It is very nearly possible to declare the victory yours

28–9 **foes ... us**: soldiers in Macbeth's army who 1 fight on our side; or 2 deliberately strike so as to miss us

THINK ABOUT for GCSE

Performance and staging

• What problems might be encountered in staging the fight sequences in Act 5 Scene 7? Think about, for example, what you would do with Young Siward's body, as his father does not see it when he enters.

Structure and form

• What are the dramatic effects of having the scene constantly switching from Dunsinane to the surrounding countryside in this Act?

I sheathe again undeeded. There thou shouldst be!   **20**
By this great clatter, one of greatest note
Seems bruited. Let me find him, Fortune! –
And more I beg not.

Exit. Battle-noise continues.

Enter Malcolm, *with* Siward.

SIWARD   This way, my lord! – The castle's gently rendered.
The tyrant's people on both sides do fight;   **25**
The noble thanes do bravely in the war. –
The day almost itself professes yours,
And little is to do.

MALCOLM   We have met with foes
That strike beside us.

SIWARD   Enter, sir, the castle.

Exeunt. Trumpet calls: battle-noise continues.

Act 5 Scene 8

In this scene ...

• Macbeth finally encounters Macduff, and is killed.

Macbeth finally faces Macduff, who destroys Macbeth's confidence by revealing that he was not born of a woman in the usual way, but by a Caesarean operation. Shocked by this news, Macbeth at first refuses to fight him.

THINK ABOUT for GCSE

Characterisation

• What are Macbeth's thoughts at this point about (a) life and death (lines 1 to 3); and (b) fighting Macduff (lines 4 to 6)?

• What do you think Macbeth now feels about the Witches and their predictions?

1–2 **play ... sword**: i.e. commit suicide as defeated Roman soldiers sometimes did

2 **lives**: living enemies
gashes: wounds

4 **Of all men else**: More than all other men

5 **charged**: weighed down

6 **blood of thine**: your family's blood

8 **Than ... out**: than words can say
Thou ... labour: You're wasting your efforts

9 **intrenchant**: uncuttable

10 **keen**: sharp
impress: cut

11 **vulnerable crests**: helmets of men who can be wounded

13 **Despair thy charm**: Give up the hope offered by the magic spell

14 **angel**: evil spirit

16 **Untimely ripped**: i.e. delivered prematurely, by a Caesarean operation

18 **cowed ... man**: disheartened me

19 **juggling**: deceiving

20 **palter ... sense**: cheat us with double meanings

21–2 **That ... hope**: who sound as though they are keeping their word, but then dash our hopes

The battlefield.

Enter MACBETH.

MACBETH   Why should I play the Roman fool, and die
On mine own sword? Whiles I see lives, the gashes
Do better upon them!

Enter MACDUFF.

MACDUFF   Turn, hell-hound! Turn!

MACBETH   Of all men else I have avoided thee. –
But get thee back, my soul is too much charged   5
With blood of thine already.

MACDUFF   I have no words:
My voice is in my sword – thou bloodier villain
Than terms can give thee out!

They fight.

MACBETH   Thou losest labour.
As easy may'st thou the intrenchant air
With thy keen sword impress, as make me bleed.   10
Let fall thy blade on vulnerable crests:
I bear a charmèd life, which must not yield
To one of woman born.

MACDUFF   Despair thy charm! –
And let the angel whom thou still hast served
Tell thee: Macduff was from his mother's womb   15
Untimely ripped.

MACBETH   Accursèd be that tongue that tells me so! –
For it hath cowed my better part of man.
And be these juggling fiends no more believed
That palter with us in a double sense –   20
That keep the word of promise to our ear,
And break it to our hope! – I'll not fight with thee.

Rather than surrender to Malcolm, Macbeth continues to fight and is killed by Macduff.

24 **show … time**: a famous public spectacle

25 **monsters**: strange creatures

26 **Painted upon a pole**: i.e. Macbeth's picture will be hung up
underwrit: with writing underneath

29 **baited … curse**: taunted and cursed by the mob

31 **thou opposed being**: even if you, the man fighting me, are

32 **try the last**: fight to the end

33 **Lay on**: Come on, start fighting again

34 **Hold, enough**: Stop, I give in

THINK ABOUT for GCSE

Performance and staging

• In some productions Macbeth and Macduff go off fighting and Macbeth is killed off-stage. His severed head is then brought on in Act 5 Scene 9. If you were the director, would you have killed Macbeth on-stage or off? Would you make the same decision in a film?

MACDUFF   Then yield thee, coward –
                And live to be the show and gaze o' th' time.
                We'll have thee, as our rarer monsters are,   25
                Painted upon a pole, and underwrit,
                'Here may you see the tyrant'.

MACBETH   I will not yield
                To kiss the ground before young Malcolm's feet,
                And to be baited with the rabble's curse.
                Though Birnam wood be come to Dunsinane,   30
                And thou opposed being of no woman born –
                Yet I will try the last. Before my body
                I throw my warlike shield. Lay on, Macduff! –
                And damned be him that first cries 'Hold, enough!'

*Exeunt, fighting on. Noise of battle comes to a climax, then
fades. They re-enter still fighting, and* MACBETH *is killed.*

Exit MACDUFF, *dragging away the body.*

In this scene ...

• Malcolm and his supporters are victorious. He rewards the lords and invites them to his coronation.

Siward expresses pride that his son died bravely.

1 **I would**: I wish

2 **must go off**: have to die

3 **So ... bought**: i.e. we have won a great victory with little loss of life

5 **a soldier's debt**: i.e. he paid with his life

7 **The which ... confirmed**: and no sooner had he confirmed his manhood by his bravery

8 **the ... fought**: the front of the fighting from which he didn't retreat

12 **before**: on the front of his body

14 **hairs**: wordplay on 'hairs' and 'heirs'

16 **knell is knolled**: funeral bell has tolled

THINK ABOUT for GCSE

Themes and issues

• In what ways might Siward's reaction to his son's death contribute to our understanding of **manhood** in this play?

18 **parted well**: died well
    paid his score: settled his account

19 **newer comfort**: better, more comforting news

Dunsinane: in the castle courtyard.

Trumpet fanfare. Enter Malcolm *and* Siward, *with* Ross, Lennox, Menteith, Caithness, *and* Angus. *Soldiers follow, with drum and banners.*

Malcolm	I would the friends we miss were safe arrived.
Siward	Some must go off. And yet, by these I see,
	So great a day as this is cheaply bought.
Malcolm	Macduff is missing, and your noble son.
Ross	Your son, my lord, has paid a soldier's debt.

5

He only lived but till he was a man –
The which no sooner had his prowess confirmed
In the unshrinking station where he fought,
But like a man he died.

Siward	Then he is dead?
Ross	Ay, and brought off the field. Your cause of sorrow

10

Must not be measured by his worth, for then
It hath no end.

Siward	Had he his hurts before?
Ross	Ay, on the front.
Siward	Why then, God's soldier be he!

Had I as many sons as I have hairs,
I would not wish them to a fairer death.

15

And so, his knell is knolled.

Malcolm	He's worth more sorrow,
	And that I'll spend for him.
Siward	He's worth no more.

They say he parted well, and paid his score:
And so, God be with him! – Here comes newer
    comfort.

Macduff enters with Macbeth's severed head. Malcolm rewards the loyal lords by giving each of them the new title of earl. He invites everyone to his coronation at Scone.

THINK ABOUT for GCSE

Performance and staging

• Malcolm's final speech seems to suggest that all will now be well, but modern productions often take a different line. If you were the director, how might you show each of the following very different interpretations in the final moments of the play: (a) that there will now be peace and happiness in Scotland; (b) that Malcolm will not be strong enough to prevent civil war from breaking out; (c) that Malcolm will himself prove to be a tyrant; and (d) that Fleance is waiting to take over, as the Witches prophesied he would?

21 **usurper**: someone who forces a rightful king off his throne and takes his place
The time: The world (our time and country)
22 **compassed ... pearl**: surrounded by your kingdom's finest noblemen
23 **That ... minds**: i.e. I am speaking their thoughts
27 **reckon ... loves**: reward you individually for your love and loyalty
28 **make ... you**: so that I'm no longer in debt to you
29 **Henceforth**: from this time onwards
31 **Which ... time**: which ought to be given a new start in this new era
32 **As**: such as
33 **watchful tyranny**: i.e. Macbeth's spies
34 **Producing forth**: bringing out of hiding
ministers: agents
36–7 **by ... life**: killed herself violently
37–8 **needful ... us**: other necessary matters demand my attention
38 **by ... Grace**: with God's help
39 **measure ... place**: the proper order, at the right time and place

Enter MACDUFF, *with* MACBETH*'s head on a pole.*

MACDUFF	(*To* MALCOLM) Hail, King! – for so thou art. Behold where stands
	Th' usurper's cursèd head. The time is free!
	I see thee compassed with thy kingdom's pearl,
	That speak my salutation in their minds –
	Whose voices I desire aloud with mine. –
	Hail, King of Scotland!
ALL	Hail, King of Scotland!

20

25

Trumpet fanfare.

MALCOLM	We shall not spend a large expense of time
	Before we reckon with your several loves,
	And make us even with you. My thanes and kinsmen,
	Henceforth be earls, the first that ever Scotland
	In such an honour named. What's more to do,
	Which would be planted newly with the time, –
	As calling home our exiled friends abroad
	That fled the snares of watchful tyranny;
	Producing forth the cruel ministers
	Of this dead butcher and his fiend-like queen,
	Who, as 'tis thought, by self and violent hands
	Took off her life; – this, and what needful else
	That calls upon us, by the grace of Grace,
	We will perform in measure, time and place.
	So thanks to all at once, and to each one –
	Whom we invite to see us crowned at Scone.

30

35

40

Trumpets sound again. Exeunt.

Macbeth was first performed in 1606 and it is a play that very much reflects the issues and events of the time it was written. In particular, it seems to have been written with a specific king in mind. In 1603 King James VI of Scotland succeeded Queen Elizabeth I. He became King James I of England and was the first monarch of both Scotland and England. He is a focus of the play in a number of ways.

SCOTLAND AND JAMES' ANCESTORS
Macbeth is set in Scotland and many of the characters in the play are James' ancestors. In Shakespeare's play the actions of Banquo, James' ancestor, are contrasted with the murderous Macbeth's. Both hear the Witches' prophecies but they react in very different ways.

When Malcolm creates Scotland's first earls at the end of the play, audiences would have been reminded of James's own generosity when he became King in handing out honours and titles.

KINGSHIP AND LOYALTY
Macbeth explores the importance of kingship and loyalty. In Shakespeare's England the king was widely believed to be God's representative on Earth, at the head of the 'natural' order. To murder a king was therefore the ultimate crime – one that could have only 'unnatural' results. When Macbeth murders Duncan, the natural world is immediately turned upside-down. The sun does not rise and Duncan's horses eat each other. Such events continue throughout the play and it is clear how serious the consequences of killing a king are.

THE GUNPOWDER PLOT
Some of the themes and issues in *Macbeth* are related to the Gunpowder Plot – the attempt in 1605 to blow up the King (James I) and Parliament (the government). In the trials that followed, a conspirator called Father Garnet became notorious for 'equivocating' (telling half-truths). *Macbeth* was written in the same year as Garnet's trial and as a result has a lot to say about equivocation. The Witches constantly tell Macbeth half-truths, and the Porter admits an imaginary equivocator to hell.

WITCHCRAFT

The Witches play a significant part in *Macbeth* and this would have interested James I. He was an expert on witchcraft, having written a book on the subject called *Demonologie*. The book described witches' powers of predicting the future, defying normal physical laws, affecting the weather, cursing their enemies, using 'familiar' spirits in the shape of animals, and taking demonic possession of innocent people. Shakespeare's Weird Sisters do many of these things.

While James was still King of Scotland, over 300 people accused of being witches were tortured to make them confess that they were conspiring against the King. James sometimes took part in the trials himself. In Elizabeth's England, hundreds of people (nearly all women) had been executed as witches.

In Shakespeare's time, people might have seen witchcraft and its effects in the world around them – a sickly child, a failed crop, a lost business deal. They would also have recognised the signs of someone possessed by demons – a trance-like state, actions that were out of character, hallucinations, and the inability to sleep. All of these they would see in the character of Macbeth.

Macbeth was written for performance in the Globe playhouse, the famous theatre on the south bank of the river Thames in London in which Shakespeare's acting company, the King's Men, was based.

What we know about the staging of plays in the Globe four hundred years ago comes mainly from the evidence of plays, like *Macbeth*, that we know were performed there. Sometimes other evidence helps, such as theatre-builders' contracts, lists of expensive costumes and props, or, less commonly, eye-witness accounts of visits to the theatre in Shakespeare's time. One such audience member, who saw *Macbeth* in 1611, records being impressed by the Witches, who would have been played by men in Shakespeare's time. And he was even more impressed by Act 3 Scene 4 where the ghost of the murdered Banquo interrupts Macbeth's royal feast. When Macbeth stood to drink to Banquo, the ghost 'came and sat down in his chair behind him.' And when Macbeth turned to sit, the bloodstained ghost glared up at him, and Macbeth 'fell into a great passion of fear and fury...'.

Banquo's ghost may have had some distance to move, eerily, when it 'disappeared'. The stage of the Globe was big (about 13 metres wide by 9 metres deep), and the action on it would have been continuous, with no intervals between Acts or scenes. No scenery or stage-lighting, as we think of them, was used. The play's language would have been enough to suggest places and settings to the imagination of its audience. Burning torches, often used in *Macbeth*, were not for lighting, but to tell the audience, in the open-air afternoon daylight of the Globe, that it was watching a 'night-time' scene. When Duncan approaches Macbeth's castle in Act 1 Scene 6, the 'castle' would have been only the decorated rising wall of the dressing-room at the back of the stage, with its two main entrances. Costumes, such as indoor or outdoor dress, armour or casual clothing, would also have signalled different settings and kinds of character for spectators.

When the murderers attack Banquo and Fleance in Act 3 Scene 3, they may well have hidden behind the two great oak pillars which supported the canopy over the stage known as 'the heavens'. And when the Witches' cauldron sinks from sight after producing its 'apparitions' in Act 4 Scene 1, it would have descended through the main trap-door in the stage into the hidden under-stage area, known as 'hell'. The stage itself, between 'heaven' and 'hell', represented our world as a kind of 'middle-earth'.

Actors on the stage, especially comic characters or specialist clowns, might sometimes play directly with spectators in the yard. The Porter in Act 2 Scene 3 of *Macbeth*, for example, might have picked on particular spectators with his invitations to 'Hell' – and when he departs saying, 'I pray you, remember the Porter', he was probably asking not just for a tip, but for applause for his hungover, drunken comic routine.

Staging in Shakespeare's theatre may seem crude or simple by modern standards, but it was in fact very flexible and effective in playing to the imaginations of its audiences. The 'special effects' in *Macbeth*, which included a frighteningly visible blood-spattered ghost and apparitions rising out of 'hell' through a cauldron, were impressively 'state of the art' for their time. And those who saw them in the Globe were prepared to use their imaginations to engage with the language, fears and dangers of the play.

A play in performance at the reconstruction of Shakespeare's Globe

As with all of Shakespeare's plays, there is no single 'correct meaning' of *Macbeth*. Different people interpret it in different ways, and new meanings are found every time it is performed. But there are some basic questions that any director of this play has to address. Three of the most important are:

- When the play begins is Macbeth already a bad man who provides a ready source of evil for the Witches to tap into? Or is he just a weak-willed man, who is manipulated by the Witches?
- As the play ends is Scotland likely to have a free and happy time under King Malcolm? Or can it expect further troubles?
- What time and place should the play be set in to get the chosen interpretation across to the audience?

MACBETH AND THE WITCHES

Many directors have taken the view that it is the Witches who are in control, luring Macbeth to evil for their own ends. This can make very exciting and dramatic theatre, and is the interpretation taken by three major productions (all available on video). Two are films made for cinema, directed by Orson Welles (1948) and Roman Polanski (1971). The third is Gregory Doran's 1999 RSC production.

Orson Welles makes it clear from the opening shots of his 1948 film that the Witches are in charge. As they chant 'Fair is foul ...', they make a hideous clay doll of Macbeth and, at the moment that Macduff kills Macbeth in Act 5 Scene 8, the film cuts to a shot of the doll having its head sliced off. To underline that the Witches have been in control throughout, the final scene is a long shot of Macbeth's castle. As the camera pulls back, the Witches come into view, gazing at the distant castle. Their final words are 'Peace! – the charm's wound up', a line borrowed from Act 1 Scene 3.

Roman Polanski takes a similar approach. His 1971 film opens on a deserted beach where the Witches are burying a severed hand holding a dagger. They depart and the place where they have cast their spell becomes the scene for the battle in which Macbeth and Banquo defeat the rebels. As soon as Macbeth meets the Witches, he seems to come under their spell. When he returns to them in Act 4, he willingly drinks the potion they have brewed for him.

When **Gregory Doran**'s 1999 RSC production was filmed for television, the disruptive power of the Witches could be seen in the fact that they caused interference on the cameras. The opening scene was filmed in a strange green light and the picture looked as though it had not been properly tuned in.

However **Trevor Nunn**'s 1976 RSC production (available on video) took a slightly different view. It opened by showing how powerful the Witches were as a force of evil opposing good: Duncan and his men were trying to pray, but their words were drowned out by a terrible howling from the Witches. Macbeth, though, was shown as a man whose problems were deep inside his mind and, although the Witches had some control over him, as they always do, you felt that the evil was more within the man himself. For example, at the point where Banquo's ghost appears in Act 3 Scene 4, Macbeth simply stared, shaking in horror, at an empty space. There was nobody sitting there, but the audience knew exactly what it was that he could see. This interpretation was helped by making the character of Lady Macbeth a powerful and terrifying figure who seemed to have at least as much control over Macbeth as the Witches did.

THE ENDING

When we read Malcolm's final speech in the text, the most obvious interpretation of the ending is that all will now be well. Scotland seems to have a good, strong King who is starting his reign sensibly by rewarding the nobles who have supported him. **Orson Welles**'s 1948 film follows this interpretation with a powerful Malcolm cheered enthusiastically by his new earls. However, many directors in recent years have taken a different view of the ending. **Trevor Nunn**'s 1976 RSC production, for example, ended with Malcolm and Macduff sitting in silence, worn out and shocked by the horrors they had been involved in. Their stunned reactions made the audience feel that, though Malcolm would be a good king, the evil would take a long time to wash away.

Polanski took a more dramatic view of the ending. His 1971 film ended with a shot of a single horseman riding across the moors to Malcolm's coronation. Suddenly the rider reigns in his horse. He has heard strange, unearthly musical sounds which we have come to associate with the Witches. He dismounts, and as he descends the rocky hillside to find the Witches, we realise that the horseman is Donalbain, Malcolm's brother. The cycle of killing and evil is about to start all over again.

Gregory Doran's 1999 RSC production seemed to have ended with Malcolm's speech. But suddenly the audience was aware of a strange noise, and at one side of the stage they saw the young Fleance, watching intently and rattling the magic token that the Witches had earlier given to Macbeth. Clearly Fleance was now in the Witches' power and would plot to overthrow Malcolm. This interpretation fits Shakespeare's script well as Banquo is told by the Witches in Act 1 Scene 3 that he will be father to a line of kings. Shakespeare doesn't tell us how that prediction comes true, but some directors take the view that Fleance will now have to overthrow Malcolm. **Dominic Cooke**'s 2004 RSC production ended with everyone leaving the stage except Fleance. As he stood there, deep in thought, the Witches crawled out of the darkness towards him.

THE SETTING

A director has to think carefully about when and where to set a production of *Macbeth*. Should the play be set in Shakespeare's own time, for example, with the actors dressed in Jacobean costume? Should it be in modern dress, or possibly set in a period between Shakespeare's time and our own? Recent productions have been set in times and places ranging from the eleventh century, when the historical Macbeth lived, to the modern day, and in places as different as eighteenth century Scotland and medieval Japan.

A modern setting has the obvious attraction that it can speak directly to today's audience. Modern-setting productions often include topical visual jokes. The 1995 **Birmingham Repertory Theatre** production included a Porter who appeared reading a TV listings magazine with a front-cover photograph of Hugh Grant. The Porter's humour is often difficult to get across to today's audience and a modern setting can make the character and his jokes easier to understand.

The 1972 **National Theatre** production took a very different approach and set the play in Shakespeare's own time. One scene even had traitors' heads stuck on poles. This setting helped the audience to understand what it might have been like to see a story about killing a king acted in public less than a year after James I himself had narrowly escaped being assassinated by the Gunpowder Plot.

ASSESSMENT OF SHAKESPEARE IN YOUR ENGLISH LITERATURE GCSE

All students studying GCSE English Literature have to study at least six texts, three of which are from the English, Welsh or Irish literary heritage. These texts must include prose, poetry and drama, and in England this must include a play by Shakespeare.

The four major exam boards: AQA, Edexcel, WJEC and OCR, include Shakespeare as part of their specifications for English Literature. All the exam boards offer controlled assessment to assess their students' understanding of Shakespeare, although some offer a traditional examination as an alternative option, or as one element of the assessment.

This section of the book offers guidance and support to help you prepare for your GCSE assessment on Shakespeare. The first part (pages 200–2) is relevant to all students, whichever exam board's course you are taking. The second part (pages 203–22) is board-specific, and you should turn to those pages that are relevant to your exam board. Your teacher will advise you if you are unsure which board you are working with.

WHAT YOU WILL BE ASSESSED ON

In your English Literature GCSE you will be marked on various Assessment Objectives (AOs). These assess your ability to:

- **AO1: respond to texts critically and imaginatively; select and evaluate relevant textual detail to illustrate and support interpretations**
  This means that you should show insight and imagination when writing about the text, showing understanding of what the author is saying and how he or she is saying it; and use quotations or direct references to the text to support your ideas and point of view.

- **AO2: explain how language, structure and form contribute to writers' presentation of ideas, themes and settings**
  This means that you need to explain how writers use language (vocabulary, imagery and other literary features), structure and form (the 'shape' of the text) to present ideas, themes and settings (where the action takes place).

- **AO3: make comparisons and explain links between texts, evaluating writers' different ways of expressing meaning and achieving effects**
  This means that you compare and link texts, identifying what they have in common and looking at how different writers express meaning and create specific effects for the reader/audience.

- **AO4: relate texts to their social, cultural and historical contexts; explain how texts have been influential and significant to self and other readers in different contexts and at different times**
  This means that, where it is relevant, you need to show awareness of the social, cultural and historical background of the texts; explain the influence of texts on yourself and other readers in different places and times.

You will also be assessed on the **Quality of your Written Communication**. This means you need to ensure that: your text is legible and your spelling, punctuation and grammar are accurate so that the meaning is clear; you choose a style of writing that is suitable for the task; you organise information clearly and logically, using specialist words where relevant.

Not all exam boards assess all the AOs as part of the English Literature Shakespeare task. Here is a summary:

Exam Board	Unit	AO1	AO2	AO3	AO4
AQA	Unit 3 CA	✓	✓	✓	✓
	Unit 4 Exam	✓	✓		
Edexcel	Unit 3 CA		✓	✓	
WJEC	Unit 3 CA	✓	✓	✓	
OCR	Unit 1 CA	✓			

WHAT IS CONTROLLED ASSESSMENT?

Controlled assessment is a way of testing students' knowledge and ability. It differs from an examination in that you will be given the task in advance so you can research and prepare for it, before sitting down to write a full response to it under supervised conditions.

Exam boards differ in the detail of their controlled assessment rules, so do check them out in the board-specific section. However, the general stages of controlled assessment are as follows:

1. **The task**
   Every year exam boards either set a specific task or offer a choice. Your teacher might adapt one of the tasks to suit you and the resources available. You will be given this task well in advance of having to respond to it, so you have plenty of time to prepare for it.

2. Planning and research

Your teacher will have helped you study your text and taught you how to approach the topics. He or she will now advise you on how to carry out further research and plan for your task.

- During this phase you can work with others, for example discussing ideas and sharing resources on the internet.
- Your teacher can give you general feedback during this phase, but not detailed advice.
- You must keep a record of all the source materials you use, including websites.

3. Writing up the response

This will take place under timed, supervised conditions.

- It may be split into more than one session, in which case your teacher will collect your work at the end of the session and put it away until the beginning of the next. You will not have access to it between sessions.
- You may be allowed to take an **un-annotated copy** of the text into the session.
- You may be allowed to take in some brief **notes**.
- You may be allowed access to a **dictionary** or a **thesaurus**.
- You may be allowed to produce your assessment electronically, but you will not be allowed access to the internet, email, disks or memory sticks.
- During this time, you may not communicate with other candidates. The work you produce must be entirely **your own**.
- Your teacher will advise you on how much you should aim to write.

4. Marking

Your Controlled Assessment Task will be marked by your teacher and moderated (supervised and checked) by your exam board.

General examiners' note

Remember:

- you will get marks for responding to the task, but not for writing other material that is not relevant
- you must produce an **individual** response to the task in the final assessment, even if you have discussed ideas with other students previously.

How to succeed in AQA English Literature

Your teachers will decide whether you should write about *Macbeth* in a Controlled Assessment Task (Unit 3) or an Examination (Unit 4). These two units are very different, so you need to be absolutely sure which one you are taking. If you are in any in doubt, ask your teacher.

Examiner's tip

Refer back to pages 200–1 for more about the assessment objectives you will be assessed on in Unit 3 Controlled Assessment or Unit 4 Exam.

Unit 3 Controlled Assessment Task

If you take this unit, you have to write about a Shakespeare play and one other text that your teacher will choose. It may be a novel, a selection of poetry, another play or even another Shakespeare play. The two texts will be linked in some way and you are expected to write about both.

The task

AQA will give your teacher a number of tasks to choose from. There are two main topics:

1. **Themes and ideas**

   These tasks might involve writing about power and conflict, the supernatural and fate, ambition, loyalty and treachery. For example: *Explore the ways writers present the supernatural in the texts you have studied* or *Explore the ways writers present and use ideas about loyalty in the texts you have studied.*

2. **Characterisation and voice**

   These tasks might involve writing about relationships, the presentation of good or evil characters, or characters who change in some way. For example: *Explore the ways the texts present murderers in the texts you have studied* or *Explore the ways the texts show how people can be influenced by others in the texts you have studied.*

Your response

- You have to complete a written response to ONE task. This should be about 2,000 words, but remember that it's quality not quantity that counts.

- You have FOUR hours to produce your work. Your teacher will probably ask you to complete the task over separate sessions rather than in a single sitting.

- Your teacher will give you plenty of time to prepare for the task. You can use any resources you like, but do keep a record of them (including websites). You must include a list of these at the end of your task.
- You can work in a small group to research and prepare your material but your final work must be all your own.
- Do watch different versions of the play. You can refer to the different versions when you write your response and you will be given credit for this.
- You can refer to brief notes when you are writing your response, but these must be brief. You must hand in your notes at the end of each session and on completion of the task. You can also use a copy of the play without any annotations.
- You can handwrite your response or use a word processor. You are allowed a dictionary and thesaurus or grammar and spell-check programs. You are NOT allowed to use the internet, email, disks or memory sticks when writing your response.
- You can do the Controlled Assessment Task in January or June. When you have finished, your teachers will mark your work and then send a sample from your school to AQA to be checked.

Examiner's tip
The Controlled Assessment Task is worth 25 per cent of your final English Literature mark – so it's worth doing it well.

HOW TO GET A GOOD GRADE

1. Select what you write about carefully. It is better to write a lot about a little. Concentrate on one scene in Shakespeare and one chapter in a novel or a single poem, or on two characters, one from a Shakespeare play and one from a novel.
2. Use short, relevant quotations. Every time you include a quotation, consider the language the writer has used and the probable effect on the audience.
3. Never retell the story. You and your teachers already know it. If you find yourself doing this, stop and refocus on the question.
4. Check your spellings, in particular writers' and characters' names.
5. Always remember that Macbeth, Lady Macbeth and the other characters in the play are not real. Do not write about them as if they are. They have been created by Shakespeare: he's the important person to consider.

SAMPLE CONTROLLED ASSESSMENT TASK

> Explore the ways writers present characters who are influenced by others.

Here are extracts from responses written by two students. Both are writing about the dialogue between Macbeth and Lady Macbeth in Act 1 Scene 7.

Extract 1 Grade C response

In this scene Lady Macbeth makes sure that her husband will do exactly what she wants him to do. Macbeth wants to stop the murder and says 'We will proceed no further'. He tells his wife that King Duncan has honoured him and he wants to enjoy his new importance. Lady Macbeth is having nothing of it. She's only after one thing and that's to be Queen. She calls him a coward and compares him to a cat that wants fish but doesn't want to get his paws wet. She means that Macbeth wants to be king but doesn't want to do anything dangerous to become king. Macbeth replies that he is a real man and will dare to do anything. But he is still worried about what will happen if they fail. Lady Macbeth dismisses this idea as being impossible 'we'll not fail'. By the end of the scene Macbeth has been persuaded to carry on with the plan. The audience is now waiting for the murder to be committed.

Annotations:
- Relevant textual detail
- Explains effect
- Could be developed more
- Very sudden ending – needs much more development
- Sustains explanation
- Good point with relevant quotation

Examiner's comments

- The student clearly understands some of Shakespeare's ideas and uses of language in the speech.
- Not all points are fully explained and backed up; for example, Lady Macbeth's accusation of cowardice.
- There is a general understanding of how Lady Macbeth influences her husband, although the effects on Macbeth and the audience are not considered in much detail.
- This is a Grade C response. To improve, this student needs to develop ideas in more detail and to link these details to a more thoughtful consideration of the scene.

Extract 2 Grade A response

The entry of Lady Macbeth interrupts her husband's soliloquy. The word 'side' is left unsaid although the meaning is clear: at this point of the play Macbeth is clearly presenting to the audience the concept that 'Vaulting ambition' may well bring dangers. The interruption leads to a series of fractured pentameters as Shakespeare creates tension. This is heightened both by the way questions are answered with others to create a sense of confusion and also the way in which Duncan is referred to as 'he', showing how both characters prefer euphemism to clear statement. The questions are ended by Macbeth's statement 'We will proceed no further in this business'. Again 'business' is a euphemism. Macbeth also uses 'we'. This may suggest that he believes that he and his wife are joint conspirators in the murder and are a bonded team, yet it may also suggest that Macbeth has begun to imitate Duncan's use of 'the royal we': Duncan has spoken of 'our graces towards him' in the previous scene. These have become 'Golden opinions from all sorts of people'. Macbeth believes himself to be universally admired and liked. Being held in high esteem is very important to him. Some people, for example his wife, might see that as a form of weakness.

Annotations:
- Clear, detailed statement
- Awareness of effect on audience
- Analytic use of detail
- Exploration of language
- Insight into motivation
- Insight into theme

Examiner's comments

- The student shows a clear engagement with Shakespeare's ideas and the attitudes of Macbeth.
- There is evidence of a sophisticated interpretation and a perceptive exploration of Shakespeare's use of language.
- The student has written a lot about a little but has also explored some of the themes of the text as a whole.
- This is a Grade A response.

UNIT 4 EXAMINATION

If you take Unit 4 in your AQA English Literature course then you will answer a question on a Shakespeare play in an examination. Your answer is worth 20 per cent of your total Literature mark and you will need to spend about 40 minutes on this question.

The Shakespeare question will always have **two** parts. Each is worth ten per cent of your total mark so you must spend equal time on them.

- Part (a) of each question will ask you to write about a specific extract that is printed in the exam paper. This extract may be a monologue (spoken by one character) or a part of a scene where two or more characters are talking.

- Part (b) of each question will ask you to write about the same topic but relating to a different part of the play (there will not be a printed extract in the exam paper to refer to).

SAMPLE EXAMINATION QUESTIONS AND RESPONSES

Part (a)	How does Shakespeare show Lady Macbeth's thoughts and feelings in the extract below?
	Extract: Act 1 Scene 5, lines 37–53 (page 39)
	From: The raven himself is hoarse ...
	To: ... To cry, "Hold, hold!"
Part (b)	How does Shakespeare show Lady Macbeth's feelings in a different part of the play?

Examiner's tip

The first part of each question asks 'How does Shakespeare . . .?' The 'how' is important. It means you must consider Shakespeare's use of language, referring to specific words and phrases and the effects these create.

Here are extracts from essays by two students. Both are answering Part (a) of the question on *Macbeth*.

Extract 1 Grade C response

Explanation of effects on audience

Sustained response to language

Appropriate comment on language

Appropriate response to character

In this soliloquy Lady Macbeth is already planning the murder of Duncan. She mentions that the raven is hoarse. A raven was thought to be a messenger of death. The audience would therefore immediately understand that she meant to murder Duncan. She then asks that she should stop being a woman and have her milk replaced by a bitter poison so that she can become really evil. She calls upon the 'murdering ministers'. The alliteration gives the phrase emphasis. She also asks for 'thick night' which means that nobody will ever see the murder. She also mentions heaven and wants it not to see what she is doing. She is clearly an evil woman who is determined to murder the king.

Examiner's comments

- The ideas here are expressed clearly and appropriately.
- The response explains the first of the images and considers the effect this would have on the audience.
- The response is sustained as it provides other examples of Shakespeare's use of language. However, comments on these examples are not developed.
- This is a Grade C response. To improve, this student must try to develop ideas in more detail and to link details to an interpretation of the speech.

Extract 2 Grade A response

In this soliloquy the audience is given a lesson in ruthlessness. Lady Macbeth, dripping irony, declares that the news of Duncan's imminent arrival is 'great'. She then fantasises about him being greeted by a raven, thought at the time to be an omen of death, whose 'croak' is 'hoarse'. The extended use of onomatopoeia and the repeated 'r' sounds produce a sinister effect: it is as if a life is being ground out. Lady Macbeth speaks of Duncan's 'entrance' as if he were a mere actor and she the all-powerful writer who would ensure that his entrance was indeed fatal. Her sense of her own power is also evident in the phrase 'under my battlements'. Duncan is given a subservient position (he is 'under her battlements' rather than walking through her gates, which may also carry an implication that he will be buried there) and Lady Macbeth uses 'my'. The use of the first person singular shows that she is clearly thinking of herself as the chatelaine in complete control of her castle and everything that might take place there: her husband is unconsidered – nothing but a tool in her hands. However, in terms of displaying a chilling desire to be the perfect murderess, a killing machine to rival her soldier husband, Lady Macbeth has only just begun.

Annotations:
- Analytic use of detail
- Clear interpretation
- Good analysis of language
- Exploration of ideas
- Insight and interpretation

Examiner's comments

- In this response the ideas are expressed cogently and persuasively and text references are apt.
- There is evidence of imagination in the development of the interpretation and there is a confident exploration of Shakespeare's use of language.
- The student has written a lot about a little but has also managed to explore some of the themes of the text as a whole.
- This is a Grade A response.

How to succeed in Edexcel English Literature

The response to Shakespeare in Edexcel GCSE English Literature is a Controlled Assessment Task. You must produce your work at school or college under supervision and within two hours, although you may do some preparation for it in advance.

The task

The task will ask you to compare and make links between your own reading of the Shakespeare text and an adaptation. The adaptation can be a film, TV production, musical, graphic novel, audio version or a cartoon, but all must be based on the original play. The task will focus on **one** of the following aspects of the play:

- **Characterisation**
  For example: a study of the importance and development of one of the main characters in the play.

- **Stagecraft**
  For example: looking at ways in which the decisions taken about the staging and set influence the production.

- **Theme**
  For example: following how the action of the play is affected by a central theme such as kingship, fate or ambition.

- **Relationships**
  For example: considering how a powerful relationship between two main characters is influential in shaping the course of events.

Note that your answer should include some discussion of dramatic devices. These include a range of theatrical techniques and styles used by the playwright to create a particular effect on the audience, such as soliloquies, monologues; juxtaposition and contrast; use of dramatic irony; use of the stage and props; actions and reactions.

Preparing your response

When preparing, you will be able to use a range of resources available at your centre, which may include the internet, TV, videos and film, live performances and notes made in class.

You must complete your tasks individually, without intervention or assistance from others. However, you will be able to use:

- copies of the text without any annotations written in them
- notes (bullet or numbered points), but not a prepared draft or continuous phrases/sentences or paragraphs)
- a dictionary or thesaurus
- grammar or spell-check programs.

Examiner's tip

If possible, see several different adaptations of *Macbeth* and compare the ways they treat the story and characters.

How to get a good grade

To get a good mark in this response, it is important that you:

- respond to the chosen drama text critically and imaginatively
- make comparisons and explain links with your own reading
- look at different ways that a production or adaptation expresses ideas
- consider what Shakespeare means and how he achieves his effects
- support your ideas by including evidence from the words of the play.

Activities

The following approaches will help you to explore *Macbeth* in preparation for the controlled assessment.

Activity 1: Characterisation

Draw up a page with two columns, one for each of two characters. List key headings under which to note down your ideas about each character, for example, contrasting characteristics such as: strength/weakness; love/hate; trust/suspicion; self-control/lack of control. Do the same for the chosen characters in the adaptation.

Activity 2: Stagecraft

In a group, plan the production of a performance of *Macbeth*. Give each member of the group a non-acting role in the production, such as being responsible for production, costume and make-up, props, lighting, sound, or set design. Decide on the three most important decisions or tasks that each member has to undertake, and make notes on each.

Activity 3: Theme

As you study *Macbeth*, decide on two important themes and note down moments in the play that deal with these. Give brief references from the text that support them.

Activity 4: Relationships

Divide a page in two, with one heading for 'Macbeth' and one for 'Lady Macbeth'. Note down your key ideas, supporting them with brief references. Consider both the positive aspects of their relationship and the negative. Compare your ideas from reading the play with how the relationship is shown in a performance or adaptation.

SAMPLE CONTROLLED ASSESSMENT TASK

> Choose one central character in the Shakespeare drama text you have
> studied. Compare your reading of the character with the presentation of the
> same character in an adaptation. Use examples from the text.

Here are extracts from essays by two candidates who had each watched
the BBC animated version *'Shakespeare: the Animated Tales – Macbeth'*.
They had then compared this with their own reading of the play.

Extract 1 Grade C response

[A clear, appropriate start]

Macbeth goes through many changes in this play. When we first
meet him, he is seen as a hero who has won a fight for his
King but because of his ambition, he becomes a villain and a killer.
Shakespeare has to make us see with his words how Macbeth
can get to be damned like the traitor, the Thane of Cawdor.
Different things move Macbeth along the road to his doom, like
his wife telling him 'Look like the innocent flower / But be the
serpent under 't' and his meeting with the Witches that tells him
he will be King. However, Shakespeare shows us that Macbeth
had flaws to start with and had black and deep desires.

[This needs more explanation]

[A sound point but not fully developed]

In the animated film, they can make the character of Macbeth
look as dark as they want as well, to reflect the words. When
Macbeth is made new Thane of Cawdor, his face is hard and
dark, but Malcolm is shown lit up bright and white like an angel.
The animation also helps us to see where things are in Macbeth's
mind, like when he is told by the witches he can become King,
a crown is shown hovering above his head. Also, when he says
'What hands are here?' the hands are glowing red, which shows he
is already being affected by guilt. However, although he is guilty,
when the King's death is announced ('Horror! Horror!'), at that
moment, Macbeth's face stays totally calm, unlike everyone else's.
He has already changed so much.

[Better to refer to the animated version earlier]

[Good example linking to Macbeth's character]

[Awareness of changes in Macbeth during the play]

Examiner's comments

- There is a sound understanding of important aspects of the animated version and this is compared appropriately with Shakespeare's text.
- Comments are clear and focused.
- The quotations are appropriate, with sound explanations.
- For a higher grade, the student needs to develop points more fully and ensure that the points from the animated version are related back closely to the original text.
- This is a Grade C response.

Extract 2 Grade A response

Recognises limitations of the medium

Understands different effects achievable through animation

Although a short animated version of the play necessarily lacks some complexities of Shakespeare's character, great pains have been taken to reflect the mental and physical changes in Macbeth. Visual clues in the animation represent the conflicts Macbeth suffers. When we first meet Macbeth, in both versions, he is a hero, but his rapid fall from grace to become a murderer and a traitor has to be believable. Thus, when we see Macbeth meeting the Weird Sisters, he already possesses the ambition ('the greatest is behind'). He is reorienting his perspective. There are visual clues as to his character in the way that Macbeth is animated. He is drawn with sharp angles and a bleak contrast between the dark hollow shadows around his eyes and their eerie paleness. Macbeth has admitted: 'Let not light see my black and deep desires'. At the same time, we see Malcolm, in contrast with Macbeth, glowing light and golden.

Good vocabulary to explain an interpretation

Shows discriminating explanation of Shakespeare's language

After Macbeth has killed Duncan, he reveals that he 'does murder sleep'. The language is brutal and resonant of further trauma. He has not only murdered the sleeping innocents, but murdered hope of ever being able to sleep innocently himself. In the animation, his guilt is transferred into the silent language of his face, and it stretches into a grotesque grimace like a mask of tragedy. Later, these ideas are enhanced as the guilt becomes madness and alters more of his mind. His shadow looms over the retreating figure of Banquo, and as he hears of Macduff fleeing, his face twists, warping hideously before it dissipates into the black figures of 'all unfortunate souls'. We see more images of the 'slaughterous thoughts' transposed so as to be read on his face.

Excellent language and interpretation

Effective analysis of the visual imagery

Examiner's comments

- This shows an excellent appreciation of how to use an adaptation to bring out interpretation of character through Shakespeare's text.
- There is perceptive analysis of key moments in the depiction of Macbeth, backed up by well-chosen links between text and animation.
- The student's language is confident, expressing a strong and effective engagement with the text and its graphic version.
- This is a Grade A response.

How to succeed in WJEC English Literature

If you are entered for English Literature GCSE (or English GCSE) you will be assessed on Shakespeare in a Controlled Assessment Task. This task will be a linked assignment, which means you need to write about the Shakespeare play you have studied, in this case, *Macbeth*, and some poetry you have studied in class. The play and poems will be linked by a theme. The possible themes are:

- love
- youth/age
- hypocrisy/prejudice
- conflict
- family and parent/child relationships
- power and ambition
- male/female relationships/role of women
- grief.

WJEC, the examination board, will specify which themes are set for the year you take the examination, and your teacher will decide which theme to focus on, according to the Shakespeare play and the poems you have studied.

Examiner's tip

Note that you will be assessed on AO1, AO2 and AO3 in this task. Refer to page 200 for details of these assessment objectives.

The task

The examination board will provide teachers with 'generic tasks'. These are general tasks that your teacher will modify to suit the class and the texts you are studying. For example, the generic task could be:

> Many plays and poems are concerned with the experience of fighting or warfare. Choose a situation where conflict and death occur in a Shakespeare play and compare it with poetry where there is a similar situation.

Your teacher will modify the task and may break it down into three sections, such as:

> Look at the way Shakespeare presents the defeat of Macbeth in the final scenes of the play.
>
> Consider the way battles/warfare are presented in some of the poems in the collection. Choose one poem to write about in particular, but make references to others.
>
> What is your personal response to the literature you have studied? In your answer, explore links between the poetry and *Macbeth*.

ACTIVITY

Think about how you would approach the task above, and write a plan for your response to the first part of the task. You might want to:

- re-read the scenes, thinking about the question as you do so
- make notes on the main events. You'll need to put the ending of the play in some sort of (brief) context: what has led up to this part of the play?
- underline, or make a note of, key words and phrases and explain how they are effective.

PREPARING YOUR RESPONSE

- You will have up to fifteen hours to prepare your response, then up to four hours to write it up.
- While you are doing your research and planning, you will have limited supervision; you may use research materials, you can work with others in your class, and your teachers will be able to give you general advice.
- Any worksheets your teacher provides to help you will be sent to the external moderator, and your teacher will have to tell the examination board about the support you have had.
- You are allowed to take an A4 sheet of notes into the final assessment with you. This will be checked to see that it is not a draft or detailed plan of any kind.

WRITING YOUR RESPONSE

- Once you start writing, you will be formally supervised (a bit like in an exam).
- You may complete the assignment over several sessions, in which case, your teacher will collect the work in at the end of each session.
- You are not allowed to discuss your work with others (other students or teachers) during this part of the assessment.
- You will be allowed to use a dictionary or thesaurus if you need to, and you may be allowed to produce the work on a word processor.
- The approximate length for this assignment is 2,000 words but quality is more important than quantity.

How to get a good grade

Be prepared to discuss characters and relationships sensitively in both the Shakespeare play and the poetry. You will be expected to show detailed knowledge of both, through well chosen, brief quotations and direct reference to the texts, in order to back up the points you make.

You should show your understanding of how the texts are written, by exploring, for example, the use of language and its effects. Do not try to simply identify literary features, for instance writing 'There are several metaphors used' or something similar. These features are only of interest if you explain why and how they are used and the effects they create.

Do explain the links and connections between the texts carefully.

Examiner's tip

Remember that you need to show your understanding of the effectiveness of specific words and phrases, so make sure you refer to the texts in close detail.

Sample Controlled Assessment Task

Look at the way Macbeth develops a greed for ambition and power in the first act of the play.

Consider the way some of the poets in the collection present power and/or ambition. Write about the way power/ambition is presented in one poem in particular, but make reference to others.

What is your personal response to the literature you have studied here? In your answer, explore the links between the poetry and *Macbeth*.

Here are extracts from essays by two students, answering the first part of the task.

Extract 1 Grade C response

Sensible focus

The first time the audience meets Macbeth he is on his way back from battle with his good friend, Banquo. We already know he is a good soldier from what the bleeding captain told King Duncan, ('brave Macbeth') and when the witches greet him as 'Thane of Glamis', 'Thane of Cawdor' and 'King hereafter' it's obvious straight away that they have sparked his ambition, because Banquo notices that he has jumped a bit ('Why do you start..?') When the witches also make predictions to Banquo, Macbeth becomes more and more impatient to know how he can become King, 'Speak, I charge you!' When Macbeth is then told that he has been made Thane of Cawdor (he is already Thane of Glamis) you can tell that the witches already have him in their powers because he says, 'The greatest is behind.' However, at that point he still thinks it might all happen without him having to do anything: 'If chance will have me king, why, chance may crown me, / Without my stir.' You can tell that he's thinking about it, though, because he says he wants to discuss what has happened with Banquo, and also he writes a letter to Lady Macbeth, telling her about the meeting with the witches and what they said. I think it is when Lady Macbeth becomes involved that Macbeth's ambition and greed for power really get going.

Apt references

Awareness of tone

Apt reference

Discussion of characters and relationships

Examiner's comments

- The points made here are sensibly focused on the task.
- There is relevant selection and some highlighting of detail.
- There is a lively engagement in the question.
- To get a higher grade, points need to be explained and developed further. For example, the quotations could be explored in more detail, with a tighter focus on the language used and its effects. Similarly, some of the points made, such as Macbeth's letter, and Lady Macbeth's response to it, could be discussed in greater detail.
- As it stands, this is a Grade C response.

Extract 2 A Grade response

Apt
references
and well-
integrated
quotations

Lady Macbeth herself acknowledges her husband's ambition
when she receives his letter telling her of the encounter
with the witches, as she says, 'Thou wouldst be great –
/ Art not without ambition', but she also recognises that
although 'fate and metaphysical aid' seem to have already
determined that Macbeth will be king, his nature, being
'too full o' the milk of human kindness / To catch the
nearest way', will stand in his way.

Indeed, there have already been indications of Macbeth's
ambition and craving for power, in the way he responded to
the meeting with the witches. Banquo remarked on how he
reacted, 'why do you start and seem to fear / Things that
do sound so fair?' and yet, when he is given the news that
King Duncan has made him Thane of Cawdor, his own words,
spoken in soliloquy, and therefore revealing his secret thoughts,
suggest his thoughts about how he may have to achieve the
third, 'greatest' prophecy are, at best, mixed:

Astute
evaluation

Good
analysis
of style
and effect

'...why do I yield to that suggestion
Whose horrid image doth unfix my hair...'

Evaluation
of character
- well
supported

Therefore, from the start of the act it is clear that
both Macbeth and Lady Macbeth acknowledge his ambition,
but both are also aware that his character is not
amenable to seizing power 'the nearest way'.

Examiner's comments

- Apt details and references from the text of the play are interwoven seamlessly with the points they support.
- There is evidence of thoughtful evaluation of character throughout.
- The reference to the soliloquy is evidence of clear appreciation of stylistic features.
- This is a Grade A response.

How to succeed in OCR English Literature

The Shakespeare task in OCR English Literature will be tested by controlled assessment. This means that you will be required to write your essay on Shakespeare, in school, under controlled conditions using notes you have made earlier.

> **Examiner's tip**
>
> You will be assessed on AO1 in your response to this Shakespeare task. Refer back to page 200 for more detail about this assessment objective.

The task and your response

- The task will ask you to show an understanding of Shakespeare's play by referring to particular scenes as they were acted and directed in either a film, staged or audio version of the play that you have watched or heard.
- Your teacher will know what the task is before you start to study the play and will give you advice on how much time you should spend preparing for it. (This time will include formal teaching, research, watching videos/live performance of the play, writing notes, etc.)
- In total, the final writing of the task is expected to take up to three hours and can be done over more than one session.
- Your final written response should be about 1,000 words.
- You will be allowed to have a clean copy, without annotations, of the play with you while writing your assessment. You can also refer to notes made in advance but these should be short bulleted points, not a full draft essay.

How to get a good grade

- Focus clearly on the terms of the question and ensure that any notes you have made also do this.
- Base your answer on the scene identified in the question but remember to show an understanding of its significance in the play as a whole.
- Show a thorough knowledge of both the written text and the performed version by using quotations and close reference to details of the performance in your response, wherever relevant. Often short quotations are as effective as long ones, particularly if you embed them fluently into your writing.

> **Examiner's tip**
>
> This Shakespeare task is worth 10 per cent of your total GCSE English Literature examination, so it is worth working hard to get a good grade.

ACTIVITIES

The following activities may help you prepare for writing your response. If possible, work in pairs or small groups so that you can discuss your ideas in full. Remember, you will know the task in advance so make bullet-point notes for reference for when you write your final essay.

Activity 1

Think about how the film/stage/audio version of *Macbeth* reflects or alters the view you formed from reading the text. For example, in the RSC production, directed by Philip Casson:

- Discuss whether Ian McKellen and Judi Dench speak the words with the same emphasis and intonations that you think they should be given?
- Do they react in the way you expect them to?
- How far does their physical appearance (for example, the costumes worn by Macbeth and Lady Macbeth) make you think differently about them?

Activity 2

Discuss how you would produce the scenes you are studying.

- Working in a small group, explore different approaches to speaking the words. Your 'actors' could experiment with different actions and gestures and then you could talk over which were most effective and why.
- How might you produce the scene with Banquo's ghost? The RSC production does not have the character represented on stage. Would you want your audience to see the ghost in your version?

Examiner's tip

Remember, there is no 'right' or 'wrong' way for a Shakespeare play to be performed and produced. However, you must be prepared to justify your own opinions with close reference to the text and to the detail of the film/ stage/audio version.

SAMPLE CONTROLLED ASSESSMENT TASK

> Remind yourself of Act 2 Scene 2 and Act 3 Scene 4 in the text and in a performed version of the play.
>
> Explore how the characters of Macbeth and Lady Macbeth are portrayed in the performed version(s) you have studied.

Here are extracts from essays by two students who had each watched the RSC film version of *Macbeth*, directed by Philip Casson.

Extract 1 Grade C response

> Better to avoid colloquial expressions

> Quite a perceptive comment on the interpretation of the part

> Tendency to summarise rather than comment

> Some awareness of the play as a whole

In the first scene Macbeth appears to be a bit unbalanced. He goes on about not being able to sleep because he thinks that he has 'murdered sleep'. The actor playing the part doesn't go over the top – he says the lines quite quietly and seems quite stunned, but the way he does it is effective as it makes you concentrate on what he's saying. Lady Macbeth seems much more in control telling him he is 'infirm of purpose'. Macbeth thinks that he will never be able to wash the blood from his hands.

In the other scene, Macbeth is dressed in military clothes and appears very confident. He smiles a lot although it looks like rather a forced smile. When Banquo's ghost appears, Macbeth falls apart and can't control himself; he has to be held up by Lady Macbeth. Again she seems in control in this scene but the next time we see her she is sleepwalking.

Examiner's comments

- This response shows that the candidate has a secure knowledge of the text of the play and what happens in it.
- There is a sensible use of appropriate quotations to support the account of the action and a sound awareness of how features of the performed version help to illustrate the implications of the text.
- To reach a higher grade, the candidate needs to make more detailed comments about the differences between Macbeth's state of mind and that of his wife and of how this is conveyed through the performance of the actors. A more developed attempt to relate their behaviour here to what happens later in the play would also help to raise the grade.
- As it stands, this is a Grade C response.

Extract 2 Grade A response

Ian McKellen's portrayal of Macbeth shows him to be eaten up by doubts and fears. He is totally wrapped up in the ramifications of the murder and his fears that he has 'murdered sleep' show how much he is obsessed with a sense of guilt. Judi Dench's Lady Macbeth appears to be more practical and in control of the situation.

Relevant quotation skilfully worked into the essay

This scene is shot in very subdued lighting and the characters are dressed in black – this links in with the play's imagery of darkness and night and emphasises the connection between the Macbeths and the 'instruments of darkness'.

Understanding of how production illustrates the imagery and themes

In the later scene Macbeth appears to be in control of events and McKellen's obsequious smiling conveys the simulation he is forced to adopt now that he has become King. Judi Dench's fixed expression reminds us of the firmness of purpose shown in the earlier scene by Lady Macbeth.

Good; simulation is a recurring and important theme

Throughout this scene we see her trying to keep things together – whispering scolding asides to her husband ('Are you a man?') and dismissing the guests. However, her facial expressions are taut and grim, indicating the tremendous strain she is under in trying to hide her guilt and prepare us for her collapse in the sleepwalking scene when she next appears in the play.

Appreciation of how an actor can convey a character's feelings and a perceptive link to later events

Examiner's comments

- This is a very good critical appreciation of well-selected details of the play and performed version.
- The candidate shows an excellent awareness of how the events of this scene relate to the wider issues of the play as a whole and of the developments in the state of mind of the two main characters in particular.
- There is a clear understanding of the text and perceptive explanation of how Shakespeare's language and imagery help to convey character.
- There is clear insight into how elements of the performed version (lighting and costumes, in particular) reinforce the effects of the language.
- This is a Grade A response.